Table of Contents

Introduction

No great venture starts without a plan. You have to make a study plan because your score depends on it. Opening up practice questions and just jumping in won't help. You need to find your strengths and weaknesses so you know where to focus your time. Doing practice tests will come later.

Creating Your Study Plan

Schedule your study time: Schedule when you will study each day and stick to it. If you have a specific amount of time set aside to work on preparing yourself, you won't have to feel the added stress of wondering if you are doing enough.

Schedule your breaks: This is just as important as scheduling your study time. You will stay motivated and focused in your studies if you know you get to go for a walk, read something else, or watch a little TV. Give yourself 10-15 minutes of break time for every hour that you study.

Short Term Goals: Set achievable goals each day (or week) for the material you will cover. This will help you stay focused on a subject or topic. There is a lot to study, and you need to be sure you are going through systematically so you don't waste time repeatedly covering the same material.

Actively Read: Don't let yourself skim through subjects. You might as well turn your brain off and stare at the wall because you will get nothing out of your time. As you read, actively think about what you have read and anticipate what you will read next. If you find yourself passively reading, take your study break.

Write things down: This means using pen and paper. The act of physically transferring ink to paper will help you solidify what you are studying in your brain. Trust us on this, it will take a little more time now while you study, but you won't waste time later going back through the same material over and over.

Study locations: Find a quiet relaxing place that you can dedicate as a "study zone." Library--good. In front of TV--bad. This location should NOT be your bed, or the couch, or anywhere else you use for sleeping, eating, or relaxing. If you sit at your desk at home or in the library, you won't be tempted to "watch TV for just a few minutes" or start nodding off because you are in bed already.

Sleep: No surprise here, you need sleep. To prepare yourself and help control your nerves when test day comes, get in the habit now of following the same routine each night and going to bed at the same time. Lying awake staring at the ceiling the entire night before the test won't do much good for your score.

<u>Practice Tests</u>: Is there any better way to prepare for a test than doing practice questions? The answer is absolutely not! The key though is you need to review the material FIRST. Don't frustrated yourself by thinking "hm, maybe I'll see what I remember without studying at all". People who do this are often very unhappy with the results, which hangs over them like a dark cloud. They keep thinking "what if I do that bad on the real test" "what if I just don't understand this stuff?". It is an unnecessary worry.

Your Plan for Test Day

<u>The Night Before</u>: Take the evening off from studying. Give your mind and body a chance to relax. Eat a healthy dinner with good carbohydrates and get a good night's rest.

<u>Food</u>: On the day of the test, avoid excess coffee and caffeine. Eat a breakfast with lots of fruits, grains, and lean protein to boost your energy and keep you full. Don't substitute sugary candies or sodas for energy.

<u>Think Positively</u>: Seriously! Imagine yourself seeing the questions and thinking confidently, "Hey, I know this answer!"

<u>Be Bold</u>: Don't second guess questions. Go with your gut instinct, but don't be careless. Make your decision and move forward. Worrying about a question from two pages ago won't help you answer the question you are on now.

<u>Don't Panic</u>: You're prepared. You worked diligently during study time and practice tests and know your own pace. Don't rush and don't worry about the clock or what anyone else is doing. This is easier said than done, but as the saying goes in sports, "you play how you practice", so if you work on good studying and test taking habits as you prepare, you'll use that same strategy on test day without even realizing it.

<u>Gum</u>: Students who chew gum during a test score higher on average than those who don't. It keeps you awake and focused. Find your favorite flavor and don't leave home without it on test day. Double check beforehand that your test taking center allows gum.

<u>Cramming</u>: Do NOT do this! It will only stress you out. And really…come on…do you think you'll actually accomplish something in a couple hours that you couldn't in the weeks you spent studying beforehand?

<u>What to Bring</u>: Along with an ID, test ticket, or other items as applicable for your exam, you SHOULD bring a watch you are familiar with and have used during your practice tests, extra batteries for your calculator, a bag or backpack for your belongings, and drinks and snacks for breaks.

<u>What to Leave at Home</u>: Scratch paper, notes and books, cell phones, MP3 players/iPods, highlighters and colored pencils, a timer (like a kitchen timer), or any type of photographic equipment or listening/recording device.

Study Tricks, Tips, and Cautions

Everyone has strengths and weaknesses, and you need to identify yours. Be honest, maybe you just aren't as good at math as you would like to be. This is your opportunity to improve. Don't fool yourself by thinking only of the concepts you know or the practice questions you got right, be critical of yourself now and work on picking up those extra points.

Only answer what is asked. Don't read between the lines. If it isn't in the question itself, don't invent a question in your mind that isn't being asked in reality. If you see something that seems really complicated or out of place, odds are they put it there just for that reason. Luckily for you, you are reading this right now, so you know not to fall for those tricks. Just answer what is asked, and that's it!

Next, we've all been there. You have answered "C" ten times in a row. That must be wrong? Is this a trick? Did you mess something up? The answer is simple: No. It's not a trick, and you didn't do anything wrong. If this happens, don't let it distract you!

You will probably come across questions you don't know the answer to. If you can, narrow your choices down to two, then make an educated guess. If there are 4 choices, your odds of getting the answer right are 50/50. If you can't narrow the answer choices to two, leave it blank, move on, and come back later if time permits. If that isn't an option for your test to revisit questions, don't lose valuable time stressing over your decision. It does no good to sit and worry for an extra minute before marking the same answer choice you would have anyway. Get it over with and move on to the next one and don't let it distract you as you work!

Develop a system for marking off the answers in the question book that you know are wrong. Do not cross off answers on the answer sheet because you don't want any stray marks getting left behind. Whatever system you adopt, be consistent in it so you don't have to think "wait, did that circle mean it's good or did that check mark mean it's good?

When should you really dig in and start studying? Base it on when you will be taking the test, rather than studying and then seeing what test dates are available.Then, work backwards to figure out how many weeks or months you have prior to the test and make a schedule. Be sure to leave an extra few weeks just in case you need a little more time.

Multiple Choice Test Taking Strategies

1) Usually, your first instinct is right. Unless you are confident you made an error or miscalculation, don't overthink your answer choices, don't go back and hem and haw over the other choices. In short, don't second guess.

2) Always read all the answer choices. Often, there will be answers that might seem correct at first glance, but are not. If you don't bother reading all the answer choices, there is a good chance you might lose points simply because you didn't give yourself the opportunity to recognize the correct answer.

3) Know the instructions and rules of the exam before sitting for the test. Know exactly what you need to do and how long you have to answer each question. Time can be your greatest enemy, so don't waste it reading instructions you could have read beforehand.

4) Know your pace. If you have 30 minutes to answer 30 questions, that can have a huge impact on your potential score if your pace is off. Even if there is no penalty for wrong answers, you have only a 25% chance at best if you are taking a wild guess and marking answers randomly as the clock ticks down.

5) Answer choices with the most information are often correct, the test makers spend more time making sure the correct answer is correct than making sure wrong answers are wrong.

6) Think before you read the answer choices. If you read the answer choices first, your thought process can be interrupted or swayed in the wrong direction. Have a possible answer in mind before reading.

7) Think "positive". Test makers typically won't have a "negative" answer choice. For example, a correct answer would not disparage or degrade someone or something. Rather, it would be a positive statement or fact.

8) "All of the above' and "none of the above" answer choices, you don't have to necessarily know if 100% of them are correct or wrong. If you see just one answer choice you know is for sure "true" or "correct", go ahead and choose "all of the above" if you are really unsure of the other choices. Vice versa for "none of the above". If you know for sure one of the answer is absolutely incorrect, but aren't 100% sure of the others but THINK they are correct, go ahead and choose none of the above.

9) Don't put undue pressure on yourself. You can psych yourself right out of a good score by worrying about potential good or bad consequences and not focusing on the task at hand. When you are on question #1 of the exam, it is too late to worry needless about "I have to ace this exam!!!"

10) Don't try to cram all your study time in at once. Studying is a marathon, not a sprint. If you study for an hour and get good quality time in, then take a break, come back for an hour later and so on, you will get much more out of the time spent than if you just powered through for hours on end.

11) Don't skip questions if you can avoid it. Errors can occur if you skip a question and test takers will often just be thinking about the question they have to go back to rather than the test question they are currently on. You can't afford to split your concentration if you want to do your best.

About the Test

The TEAS exam is three-and-a-half hours long, and is divided into the following sections:

1. **Mathematics**
   - 34 Questions: Arithmetic, Basic Geometry, and Data Interpretation.
   - 51-Minute Time Limit.

2. **English and Language Arts**
   - 34 Questions: Grammar and Word Knowledge.
   - 34-Minute Time Limit.

3. **Reading**
   - 48 Questions: Reading Comprehension.
     58-Minute Time Limit.

4. **Science**
   - 54 Questions: Biology, Chemistry, Physics, and Ecology.
     66-Minute Time Limit

Scoring

You cannot "pass" or "fail" the TEAS exam. Your score is simply indicative of your current level of comprehension. However, each school has their own entrance requirements – some are higher than others. Be sure to check with the requirements of the institutions which you want to attend.

How This Book Works

The subsequent chapters in this book are divided into a review of those topics covered on the exam. This is not intended to "teach" or "re-teach" you these concepts – there is no way to cram all of that material into one book! Instead, we are going to help you recall all of the information which you've already learned. Even more importantly, we'll show you how to apply that knowledge.

Each chapter includes an extensive review, with practice drills at the end to test your knowledge. With time, practice, and determination, you'll be well-prepared for test day.

Chapter 1: Mathematics

This chapter will cover the many subjects included in the math section of the TEAS: basic algebra, geometry, and applied math.

The Most Common Mistakes

People make mistakes all the time – but during a test, those mistakes can make the difference between an excellent score, or one which falls below the requirements. Watch out for these common mistakes that people make on the TEAS:

- Answering with the wrong sign (positive / negative).

- Mixing up the Order of Operations.

- Misplacing a decimal.

- Not reading the question thoroughly (and therefore providing an answer that was not asked for.)

- Circling the wrong letter, or filling in wrong circle choice.

If you're thinking, "Those ideas are just common sense" – exactly! Most of the mistakes made on the TEAS are simple mistakes. Regardless, they still result in a wrong answer and the loss of a potential point.

Strategies for the Mathematics Section

1. **Go Back to the Basics**: First and foremost, practice your basic skills: sign changes, order of operations, simplifying fractions, and equation manipulation. These are the skills used most on the TEAS, though they are applied in different contexts. Remember that when it comes right down to it, all math problems rely on the four basic skills of addition, subtraction, multiplication, and division. All that changes is the order in which they are used to solve a problem.

2. **Don't Rely on Mental Math**: Using mental math is great for eliminating answer choices, but ALWAYS WRITE IT DOWN! This cannot be stressed enough. Use whatever paper is provided; by writing and/or drawing out the problem, you are more likely to catch any mistakes. The act of writing things down forces you to organize your calculations, leading to an improvement in your TEAS score.

3. **The Three-Times Rule**:

    *   **Step One – Read the question**: Write out the given information.

    *   **Step Two – Read the question**: Set up your equation(s) and solve.

    *   **Step Three – Read the question:** Make sure that your answer makes sense (is the amount too large or small; is the answer in the correct unit of measure, etc.).

4. **Make an Educated Guess**: Eliminate those answer choices which you are relatively sure are incorrect, and then guess from the remaining choices. Educated guessing is critical to increasing your score.

Math Concepts Tested on the TEAS

You need to practice in order to score well on the test. To make the most out of your practice, use this guide to determine the areas for which you need more review. Most importantly, practice all areas under testing circumstances (a quiet area, a timed practice test, no looking up facts as you practice, etc.)

When reviewing, take your time and let your brain recall the necessary math. If you are taking the TEAS, then you have already had course instruction in these areas. The examples given will "jog" your memory.

The next few pages will cover various math subjects (starting with the basics, but in no particular order), along with worked examples.

Percentile

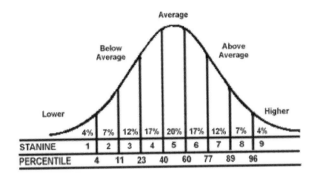

A percentile curve is simply a comparison of results relative to all other results. As you can see, if your score is a stanine of 5, you are right in the middle at the 50th percentile. This means that you did better than half of everyone else, but half did better than you. Approximately 20% of takers will fall into the stanine score range of 5.

Percentile scores do not indicate how many questions answered correctly, only how well you performed against everyone else. For example, if the score range is 90 –100, that means that everyone did very well; but those who scored a 90 are still in the stanine range of 1.

> **Example**: If you and 20% of the rest of your class scored a 95 on a test, using the chart above, would your stanine score be?

> **5** (50th Percentile).

Positive & Negative Number Rules

$(+) + (-) =$ Subtract the two numbers. Solution gets the sign of the larger number.

$(-) + (-) =$ Negative number.

$(-) * (-) =$ Positive number.

$(-) * (+) =$ Negative number.

$(-) / (-) =$ Positive number.

$(-) / (+) =$ Negative number.

Greatest Common Factor (GCF)

The greatest factor that divides two numbers.

> **Example**: The GCF of 24 and 18 is 6. 6 is the largest number, or greatest factor, that can divide both 24 and 18.

Order of Operations

PEMDAS – **P**arentheses/**E**xponents/**M**ultiply/**D**ivide/**A**dd/**S**ubtract

Perform the operations within parentheses first, and then any exponents. After those steps, perform all multiplication and division. (These are done from left to right, as they appear in the problem) Finally, do all required addition and subtraction, also from left to right as they appear in the problem.

Examples:

1. Solve $(-(2)^2 - (4 + 7))$:
   - $(-4 - 11) = -\textbf{15}$.

2. Solve $((5)^2 \div 5 + 4 * 2)$:
   - $25 \div 5 + 4 * 2$.
   - $5 + 8 = \textbf{13}$.

Probabilities

A probability is found by dividing the number of desired outcomes by the number of possible outcomes. (The piece divided by the whole.)

Example: What is the probability of picking a blue marble if 3 of the 15 marbles are blue?

$3/15 = 1/5$. The probability is **1 in 5** that a blue marble is picked.

Fractions

Adding and subtracting fractions requires a common denominator.

Find a common denominator for:

$$\frac{2}{3} - \frac{1}{5}.$$

$$\frac{2}{3} - \frac{1}{5} = \frac{2}{3}\left(\frac{5}{5}\right) - \frac{1}{5}\left(\frac{3}{3}\right) = \frac{10}{15} - \frac{3}{15} = \frac{7}{\textbf{15}}.$$

To add mixed fractions, work first the whole numbers, and then the fractions.

$$2\frac{1}{4} + 1\frac{3}{4} = 3\frac{4}{4} = \textbf{4}.$$

To subtract mixed fractions, convert to single fractions by multiplying the whole number by the denominator and adding the numerator. Then work as above.

$$2\frac{1}{4} - 1\frac{3}{4} = \frac{9}{4} - \frac{7}{4} = \frac{2}{4} = \frac{1}{2}.$$

To multiply fractions, convert any mixed fractions into single fractions and multiply across; reduce to lowest terms if needed.

$$2\frac{1}{4} * 1\frac{3}{4} = \frac{9}{4} * \frac{7}{4} = \frac{63}{16} = 3\frac{15}{16}.$$

To divide fractions, convert any mixed fractions into single fractions, flip the second fraction, and then multiply across.

$$2\frac{1}{4} \div 1\frac{3}{4} = \frac{9}{4} \div \frac{7}{4} = \frac{9}{4} * \frac{4}{7} = \frac{36}{28} = 1\frac{8}{28} = 1\frac{2}{7}.$$

Simple Interest

Interest * Principle.

Example: If I deposit $500 into an account with an annual rate of 5%, how much will I have after 2 years?

1st year: $500 + (500*.05) = 525.$

2nd year: $525 + (525*.05) = \textbf{551.25}.$

Prime Factorization

Expand to prime number factors.

Example: $104 = 2 * 2 * 2 * 13.$

Absolute Value

The absolute value of a number is its distance from zero, not its value.

So in $|x| = a$, "x" will equal "$-a$" as well as "a."

Likewise, $|3| = 3$, and $|-3| = 3$.

Equations with absolute values will have two answers. Solve each absolute value possibility separately. All solutions must be checked into the original equation.

Example: Solve for x: $|2x - 3| = x + 1$

1. Equation One: $2x - 3 = -(x + 1)$.
   - $2x - 3 = -x - 1$.
   - $3x = 2$.
   - $x = 2/3$.

2. Equation Two: $2x - 3 = x + 1$.
   - $x = 4$.

Mean, Median, Mode

Mean is a math term for "average." Total all terms and divide by the number of terms.

Find the mean of 24, 27, and 18.

$24 + 27 + 18 = 69 \div 3 = \mathbf{23}$.

Median is the middle number of a given set, found after the numbers have all been put in numerical order. In the case of a set of even numbers, the middle two numbers are averaged.

What is the median of 24, 27, and 18?

18, **24**, 27.

What is the median of 24, 27, 18, and 19?

18, 19, 24, 27 ($19 + 24 = 43$. $43/2 = \mathbf{21.5}$).

Mode is the number which occurs most frequently within a given set.

What is the mode of 2, 5, 4, 4, 3, 2, 8, 9, 2, 7, 2, and 2?

The mode would be **2** because it appears the most within the set.

Arithmetic Sequence

Each term is equal to the previous term plus x.

Example: 2, 5, 8, 11.
- $2 + 3 = 5; 5 + 3 = 8 \dots$ etc.
- $x = \mathbf{3}$.

Geometric Sequence

Each term is equal to the previous term multiplied by x.

Example: 2, 4, 8, 16.
- $x = \mathbf{2}$.

Percent, Part, & Whole

Part = Percent * Whole.

Percent = Part / Whole.

Whole = Part / Percent.

Example: Jim spent 30% of his paycheck at the fair. He spent $15 for a hat, $30 for a shirt, and $20 playing games. How much was his check? (Round to nearest dollar.)

Whole = 65 / .30 = **$217.00**.

Percent Change

Percent Change = Amount of Change / Original Amount * 100.

Percent Increase = (New Amount – Original Amount) / Original Amount * 100.

Percent Decrease = (Original Amount – New Amount) / Original Amount * 100.

Amount Increase (or **Decrease**) = Original Price * Percent Markup (or Markdown).

Original Price = New Price / (Whole - Percent Markdown [or Markup]).

Example: A car that was originally priced at $8300 has been reduced to $6995. What percent has it been reduced?

(8300 – 6995) / 8300 * 100 = **15.72%**.

Repeated Percent Change

Increase: Final amount = Original Amount * $(1 + \text{rate})^{\text{\# of changes}}$.

Decrease: Final Amount = Original Amount * $(1 - \text{rate})^{\text{\# of changes}}$.

Example: The weight of a tube of toothpaste decreases by 3% each time it is used. If it weighed 76.5 grams when new, what is its weight in grams after 15 uses?

Final amount = $76.5 * (1 - .3)^{15}$.

$76.5 * (.97)^{15}$ = **48.44 grams**.

Combined Average

Weigh each average individual average before determining the sum.

> **Example**: If Cory averaged 3 hits per game during the summer and 2 hits per game during the fall and played 7 games in the summer and 8 games in the fall, what was his hit average overall?
>
> 1. Weigh each average.
>   - Summer: $3 * 7 = 21$.
>   - Fall: $2 * 8 = 16$.
>   - Sum: $21 + 16 = 47$.
>
> 2. Total number of games: $7 + 8 = 15$.
>
> 3. Calculate average: $47/15 = \sim$ **3.13 hits/game**.

You may need to work a combined average problem with a missing term.

> **Example**: Bobbie paid an average of $20 a piece for ten shirts. If five of the shirts averaged $15 each, what was the average cost of the remaining shirts?
>
> 1. Calculate sum: $10 * 20 = 200$.
>
> 2. Calculate sub-sum #1: $5 * 15 = 75$.
>
> 3. Calculate sub-sum #2: $200 - 75 = 125$.
>
> 4. Calculate average: $125 / 5 = 25.

Ratios

To solve a ratio, simply find the equivalent fraction. To distribute a whole across a ratio:

1. Total all parts.

2. Divide the whole by the total number of parts.

3. Multiply quotient by corresponding part of ratio.

> **Example:** There are 90 voters in a room, and they are either Democrat or Republican. The ratio of Democrats to Republicans is 5:4. How many Republicans are there?
>
> 1. $5 + 4 = 9$.
>
> 2. $90 / 9 = 10$.
>
> 3. $10 * 4 = $ **40 Republicans**.

Proportions

Direct Proportions: Corresponding ratio parts change in the same direction (increase/decrease).

Indirect Proportions: Corresponding ratio parts change in opposite directions (as one part increases the other decreases).

> **Example:** A train traveling 120 miles takes 3 hours to get to its destination. How long will it take if the train travels 180 miles?

120 mph: 180 mph is to x hours: 3 hours. (Write as fraction and cross multiply.)
- $120/3 = 180/x$.
- $540 = 120x$.
- $x =$ **4.5 hours**.

Roots

Root of a Product: $\sqrt[n]{a \cdot b} = \sqrt[n]{a} \cdot \sqrt[n]{b}$.

Root of a Quotient: $\sqrt[n]{\dfrac{a}{b}} = \dfrac{\sqrt[n]{a}}{\sqrt[n]{b}}$.

Fractional Exponent: $\sqrt[n]{a^{m}} = a^{m/n}$.

Fundamental Counting Principle

(The number of possibilities of an event happening) * (the number of possibilities of another event happening) = the total number of possibilities.

> **Example**: If you take a multiple choice test with 5 questions, with 4 answer choices for each question, how many test result possibilities are there?

Solution: Question 1 has 4 choices; question 2 has 4 choices; etc.

4 *4 * 4 * 4 * 4 (one for each question) = **1024 possible test results**.

Literal Equations

Equations with more than one variable. Solve in terms of one variable first.

> **Example**: Solve for y: $4x + 3y = 3x + 2y$.

1. Combine like terms: $3y - 2y = 4x - 2x$.

2. Solve for y. $y =$ **$2x$**.

Linear Systems

A linear system requires the solving of two literal equations simultaneously. There are two different methods (Substitution and Addition) that can be used to solve linear systems.

Substitution Method: Solve for one variable first, and then substitute.

    Example: Solve for x and y: $3y - 4 + x = 0$ and $5x + 6y = 11$.

1. Solve for one variable.
   - $3y - 4 + x = 0$.
   - $3y + x = 4$.
   - $x = 4 - 3y$.

2. Substitute into second equation, and solve.
   - $5(4 - 3y) + 6y = 11$.
   - $20 - 15y + 6y = 11$.
   - $20 - 9y = 11$.
   - $-9y = -9$.
   - $y = 1$.

3. Substitute into first equation.
   - $3(1) - 4 + x = 0$.
   - $-1 + x = 0$.
   - $x = 1$.

Addition Method: Manipulate one of the equations so that when added to the other, one variable is eliminated.

    Example: Solve $2x + 4y = 8$ and $4x + 2y = 10$.

1. Manipulate one equation to eliminate a variable when added together.
   - $-2(2x + 4y = 8) = (-4x - 8y = -16)$.
   - $(-4x - 8y = -16) + (4x + 2y = 10)$.
   - $-6y = -6$.
   - $y = 1$.

2. Plug into an equation and solve for the other variable.
   - $2x + 4(1) = 8$.
   - $2x + 4 = 8$.
   - $2x = 4$.
   - $x = 2$.

The following is a typical word problem that would use a linear system to solve.

Example: Tommy has a collection of coins worth $5.20. He has 8 more nickels than quarters. How many of each does he have?

1. Set up equations.
   - Let n = nickels and q = quarters.
   - $.05n + .25q = 5.2$.
   - $n = q + 8$.

2. Substitute Equation 2 into Equation 1.
   - $.05(q + 8) + .25q = 5.2$.

3. Solve for q. You can ignore the decimal point and negative sign after this step because you are solving for number of coins.
   - $-.05(q + 8) + .25q = 5.2$.
   - $.05q + .4 + .25q = 5.2$.
   - $q = 16$.

4. Plug into the original equation.
   - $n = q + 8$.
   - $n = 24$.
   - $q = 16$.

Linear Equations

An equation for a straight line. The variable CANNOT have an exponent, square roots, cube roots, etc.

Example: $y = 2x + 1$ is a straight line, with "1" being the y-intercept, and "2" being the positive slope.

Algebraic Equations

When simplifying or solving algebraic equations, you need to be able to utilize all math rules: exponents, roots, negatives, order of operations, etc.

1. Add & Subtract: Only the coefficients of like terms.

   Example: $5xy + 7y + 2yz + 11xy - 5yz = 16xy + 7y - 3yz$.

2. Multiplication: First the coefficients then the variables.

   Example: Monomial * Monomial. (Remember: a variable with no exponent has an implied exponent of 1.)
   - $(3x^4y^2z)(2y^4z^5) = 6x^4y^6z^6$.

   Example: Monomial * Polynomial.
   - $(2y^2)(y^3 + 2xy^2z + 4z) = 2y^5 + 4xy^4z + 8y^2z$

19

Example: Binomial * Binomial.

- $(5x + 2)(3x + 3)$. Remember: FOIL (First, Outer, Inner, Last).

  First: $5x * 3x = 15x^2$.

  Outer: $5x * 3 = 15x$.

  Inner: $2 * 3x = 6x$.

  Last: $2 * 3 = 6$.

  Combine like terms: $15x^2 + 21x + 6$.

Example: Binomial * Polynomial.

- $(x + 3)(2x^2 - 5x - 2)$.

  First Term: $x(2x^2 - 5x - 2) = 2x^3 - 5x^2 - 2x$.

  Second term: $3(2x^2 - 5x - 2) = 6x^2 - 15x - 6$.

  Added Together: $2x^3 + x^2 - 17x - 6$.

Inequalities

Inequalities are solved like linear and algebraic equations, except the sign must be reversed when dividing by a negative number.

Example: $-7x + 2 < 6 - 5x$.

Step 1 – Combine like terms: $-2x < 4$.

Step 2 – Solve for x. (Reverse the sign): $x > -2$.

Solving compound inequalities will give you two answers.

Example: $-4 \leq 2x - 2 \leq 6$.

Step 1 – Add 2 to each term to isolate x: $-2 \leq 2x \leq 8$.

Step 2: Divide by 2: $-1 \leq x \leq 4$.

Solution set is **[-1, 4]**.

Exponent Rules

Rule	Example
$x^0 = 1$	$5^0 = 1$
$x^1 = x$	$5^1 = 5$
$x^a \cdot x^b = x^{a+b}$	$5^2 * 5^3 = 5^5$
$(xy)^a = x^a y^a$	$(5 * 6)^2 = 5^2 * 6^2 = 25 * 36$
$(x^a)^b = x^{ab}$	$(5^2)^3 = 5^6$
$(x/y)^a = x^a / y^a$	$(10/5)^2 = 10^2/5^2 = 100/25$
$x^a / y^b = x^{a-b}$	$5^4/5^3 = 5^1 = 5$ (remember $x \neq 0$)
$x^{1/a} = \sqrt[a]{x}$	$25^{1/2} = \sqrt[2]{25} = 5$
$x^{-a} = \dfrac{1}{x^a}$	$5^{-2} = \dfrac{1}{5^2} = \dfrac{1}{25}$ (remember $x \neq 0$)
$(-x)^a$ = positive number if "a" is even; negative number if "a" is odd.	

Permutations

The number of ways a set number of items can be arranged. Recognized by the use of a factorial ($n!$), with n being the number of items.

If $n = 3$, then $3! = 3 * 2 * 1 = 6$. If you need to arrange n number of things but x number are alike, then $n!$ is divided by $x!$.

Example: How many different ways can the letters in the word **balance** be arranged?

Solution: There are 7 letters, so $n! = 7!$ But 2 letters are the same, so $x! = 2!$ Set up the equation:

$$\frac{7 * 6 * 5 * 4 * 3 * 2 * 1}{2 * 1} = \textbf{2540 ways.}$$

Combinations

To calculate total number of possible combinations, use the formula: $n!/r! \, (n-r)!$
Where n = # of objects; and r = # of objects selected at a time.

Example: If seven people are selected in groups of three, how many different combinations are possible?

Solution:

$$\frac{7 * 6 * 5 * 4 * 3 * 2 * 1}{(3 * 2 * 1)(7 - 3)} = \textbf{210 possible combinations.}$$

Quadratics

Factoring: converting $ax^2 + bx + c$ to factored form. Find two numbers that are factors of c and whose sum is b.

Example: Factor $2x^2 + 12x + 18 = 0$.

1. If possible, factor out a common monomial: $2(x^2 - 6x + 9)$.

2. Find two numbers that are factors of 9; and also sum to -6: $2(x - \_)(x - \_)$.

3. Fill in the binomials. Be sure to check your answer and signs: $2(x - 3)(x - 3)$.

4. To solve, set each to $= 0$: $x - 3 = 0$; **$x = 3$**.

If the equation cannot be factored (there are no two factors of c that sum to $= b$), the quadratic formula is used.

$$x = \frac{-b \pm \sqrt{b^2 - 4ac}}{2a}$$

Using the same equation from the above example: $a = 2$, $b = 12$, and $c = 18$. Plug into the formula and solve. Remember there will still be two answers due to the (+) and (-) before the radical.

Graphs and Charts

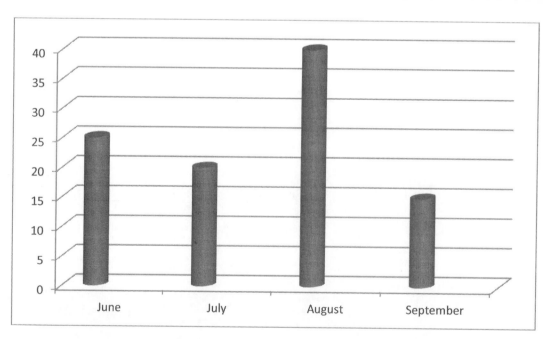

Using the above chart of ice cream sales per month, how many more sales are made in July than September? As you can see, sales in July are 20 and September sales are 15. The correct answer is therefore **5**. If you see any answer choices which are grossly incorrect – such as -10 or 20 – immediately count them out. Don't over-think graphical questions. They are typically straightforward and require only that you pay attention and don't try to answer too quickly.

Geometry

- **Acute Angle**: Measures less than 90°.

- **Acute Triangle**: Each angle measures less than 90°.

- **Obtuse Angle**: Measures greater than 90°.

- **Obtuse Triangle**: One angle measures greater than 90°.

- **Adjacent Angles**: Share a side and a vertex.

- **Complementary Angles**: Adjacent angles that sum to 90°.

- **Supplementary Angles**: Adjacent angles that sum to 180°.

- **Vertical Angles**: Angles that are opposite of each other. They are always congruent (equal in measure).

- **Equilateral Triangle**: All angles are equal.

- **Isosceles Triangle**: Two sides and two angles are equal.

- **Scalene**: No equal angles.

- **Parallel Lines**: Lines that will never intersect. Y ll X means line Y is parallel to line X.

- **Perpendicular lines**: Lines that intersect or cross to form 90° angles.

- **Transversal Line**: A line that crosses parallel lines.

- **Bisector**: Any line that cuts a line segment, angle, or polygon exactly in half.

- **Polygon**: Any enclosed plane shape with three or more connecting sides (ex. a triangle).

- **Regular Polygon**: Has all equal sides and equal angles (ex. square).

- **Arc**: A portion of a circle's edge.

- **Chord**: A line segment that connects two different points on a circle.

- **Tangent**: Something that touches a circle at only one point without crossing through it.

- **Sum of Angles**: The sum of angles of a polygon can be calculated using $(n-1)180^\circ$, when n = the number of sides.

Triangles

The angles in a triangle add up to 180°.
Area of a triangle = ½ * *b* * *h*, or ½*bh*.
Pythagoras' Theorem: $a^2 + b^2 = c^2$.

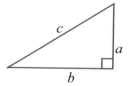

Regular Polygons

Polygon Angle Principle: $S = (n-2)180$, where S = the sum of interior angles of a polygon with *n*-sides.

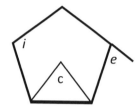

The measure of each central angle (*c*) is 360°/*n*.
The measure of each interior angle (*i*) is (*n* – 2)180°/*n*.
The measure of each exterior angle (*e*) is 360°/*n*.
To compare areas of similar polygons: $A_1/A_2 = (\text{side}_1/\text{side}_2)^2$

Trapezoids

Four-sided polygon, in which the bases (and only the bases) are parallel.

Isosceles Trapezoid: Base angles are congruent.

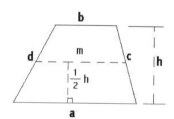

Area and Perimeter of a Trapezoid

$$m = \frac{1}{2}(a + b)$$

$$Area = \frac{1}{2} h * (a + b) = m * h$$

$$Perimeter = a + b + c + d = 2m + c + d$$

If *m* is the median then: *m* ll $\overline{AB}$ and *m* ll *CD*

Rhombus

Four-sided polygon, in which all four sides are congruent and opposite sides are parallel.

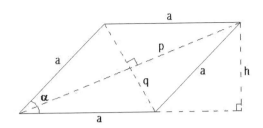

Area and Perimeter of a Rhombus

$$Perimeter = 4a$$

$$Area = a^2 \sin \alpha = a * h = \frac{1}{2}pq$$

$$4a^2 = p^2 + q^2$$

Rectangle

Area and Perimeter of a Rectangle

$$d = \sqrt{a^2 + h^2}$$

$$a = \sqrt{d^2 - h^2}$$

$$h = \sqrt{d^2 - a^2}$$

$$Perimeter = 2a + 2h$$

$$Area = a \cdot h$$

Square

Area and Perimeter of a Square

$$d = a\sqrt{2}$$

$$Perimeter = 4a = 2d\sqrt{2}$$

$$Area = a^2 = \frac{1}{2}d^2$$

Circle

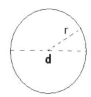

Area and Perimeter of a Circle

$$d = 2r$$

$$Perimeter = 2\pi r = \pi d$$

$$Area = \pi r^2$$

Cube

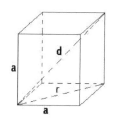

Area and Volume of a Cube

$$r = a\sqrt{2}$$

$$d = a\sqrt{3}$$

$$Area = 6a^2$$

$$Volume = a^3$$

Cuboid

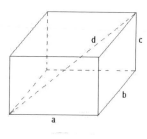

Area and Volume of a Cuboid

$$d = \sqrt{a^2 + b^2 + c^2}$$

$$A = 2(ab + ac + bc)$$

$$V = abc$$

Test Your Knowledge: Mathematics – Question Bank

Section 1:
Percent/Part/Whole; Percent Change

Section 2:
Mean, Median, Mode

Section 3:
Exponents and Roots

Section 4:
Algebraic Equations

Section 5:
Inequalities, Literal Equations, Polynomials, Binomials

Section 6:
Slope and Distance to Midpoint

Section 7:
Absolute Value Equations

Section 8:
Geometry

Section 9:
Fundamental Counting Principle, Permutations, Combinations

Section 10:
Ratios, Proportions, Rate of Change

Test Your Knowledge: Percent/Part/Whole, Percent Change

1. In a class of 42 students, 18 are boys. Two girls get transferred to another school. What percent of students remaining are girls?
   a) 14%.
   b) 16%.
   c) 52.4%.
   d) 60%.
   e) None of the above.

2. A payroll check is issued for $500.00. If 20% goes to bills, 30% of the remainder goes to pay entertainment expenses, and 10% of what is left is placed in a retirement account, then approximately how much is remaining?
   a) $150.
   b) $250.
   c) $170.
   d) $350.
   e) $180.

3. A painting by Van Gogh increased in value by 80% from year 1995 to year 2000. If in year 2000, the painting is worth $7200, what was its value in 1995?
   a) $1500.
   b) $2500.
   c) $3000.
   d) $4000.
   e) $5000.

4. "Dresses and Ties" sells a particular dress for $60 dollars. But, they decide to discount the price of that dress by 25%. How much does the dress cost now?
   a) $55.
   b) $43.
   c) $45.
   d) $48.
   e) $65.

5. A sweater goes on sale for 30% off. If the original price was $70, what is the discounted price?
   a) $48.
   b) $49.
   c) $51.
   d) $65.
   e) $52.

6. If the value of a car depreciates by 60% over ten years, and its value in the year 2000 is $2500, what was its value in the year 1990?
   a) $6000.
   b) $6230.
   c) $6250.
   d) $6500.
   e) $6600.

7. If an account is opened with a starting balance of $500, what is the amount in the account after 3 years if the account pays compound interest of 5%?
   a) $560.80.
   b) $578.81.
   c) $564.50.
   d) $655.10.
   e) $660.00.

8. A piece of memorabilia depreciates by 1% every year. If the value of the memorabilia is $75000, what will it be 2 years from now? Give the answer as a whole number.
   a) $74149.
   b) $74150.
   c) $73151.
   d) $71662.
   e) $73507.

9. A dress is marked down by 20% in an effort to boost sales for one week. After that week, the price of the dress is brought back to the original value. What percent did the price of the dress have to be increased from its discounted price?
   a) 20%.
   b) 25%.
   c) 120%.
   d) 125%.
   e) 15%.

10. A car dealer increases the price of a car by 30%, but then discounts it by 30%. What is the relationship between the final price and the original price?
   a) $.91x : x$.
   b) $.98x : x$.
   c) 1:1.
   d) $.88x : x$.
   e) $.75x : x$.

Test Your Knowledge: Percent/Part/Whole, Percent - Answers

1. **e)**

   The entire class has 42 students, 18 of which are boys, meaning 42 - 18 = 24 is the number of girls. Out of these 24 girls, 2 leave; so 22 girls are left. The total number of students is now 42 - 2 = 40.

   22/40 * 100 = 55%.

   Reminder: If you forget to subtract 2 from the total number of students, you will end up with 60% as the answer. Sometimes you may calculate an answer that has been given as a choice; it can still be incorrect. Always check your answer.

2. **b)**

   If out of the entire paycheck, 20% is first taken out, then the remainder is 80%. Of this remainder, if 30% is used for entertainment, then (.8 - .80 * .30) = .560 is left. If 10% is put into a retirement account, then (.56 - .56 * .1) = .504 is remaining. So out of $500, the part that remains is 50%, which is $252.

3. **d)**

   In 2005, the value was 1.8 times its value in 1995. So $1.8x = 7200 \rightarrow x = 4000$.

4. **c)**

   60 * (100 - 25)/100 $\rightarrow$ 60 * .75 = 45.

5. **b)**

   New price = original price * (1 – discount) $\rightarrow$ new price = 70(1-.3) = 49.

6. **c)**

   $Value_{2000}$ = Original price * (1-.6) $\rightarrow$ 2500 = .4P = 2500 $\rightarrow$ P = 6250.

7. **b)**

   Amount = $P(1 + r)^t$ = 500 * 1.05^3 = $578.81.

8. **e)**

   Final value = 75000$(1 - .1)^2$ = 73507.

9. **b)**

   If the original price of the dress was x, then the discounted price would be 0.8x. To increase the price from .8x to x, the percent increase would be (x - .8x)/.8x * 100 = 25%.

10. **a)**

    Let the original price of the car be x. After the 30% increase, the price is 1.3x.

    After discounting the increased price by 30%, it now is .7 * 1.3x = .91x. Therefore, the ratio of the final price to the original price = .91x : x.

Test Your Knowledge: Mean, Median, Mode

1. If test A is taken 5 times with an average result of 21, and test B is taken 13 times with an average result of 23, what is the combined average?
   a) 22.24.
   b) 22.22.
   c) 22.00.
   d) 22.44.
   e) 24.22.

2. A set of data has 12 entries. The average of the first 6 entries is 12, the average of the next two entries is 20, and the average of the remaining entries is 4. What is the average of the entire data set?
   a) 10.
   b) 10.67.
   c) 11.
   d) 12.67.
   e) 10.5.

3. What is the average score of 8 tests where the score for 3 tests is 55, the score for two tests is 35, and the remaining tests have scores of 70?
   a) 50.3.
   b) 52.5.
   c) 55.1.
   d) 56.0.
   e) 55.6.

4. The temperatures over a week are recorded as follows:

Day	High	Low
Monday	80	45
Tuesday	95	34
Wednesday	78	47
Thursday	79	55
Friday	94	35
Saturday	67	46
Sunday	76	54

   What is the approximate average high temperature and average low temperature during the week?
   a) 90, 50.
   b) 80, 40.
   c) 81, 45.
   d) 82, 46.
   e) 81, 47.

5. Twelve teams competed in a mathematics test. The scores recorded for each team are: 29, 30, 28, 27, 35, 43, 45, 50, 46, 37, 44, and 41. What is the median score?
   a) 37.
   b) 41.
   c) 39.
   d) 44.
   e) 45.

6. A class of 10 students scores 90, 78, 45, 98, 84, 79, 66, 87, 78, and 94. What is the mean score? What is the median score? What is the mode?
   a) 69.9, 81.5, 78.
   b) 79.9, 80, 78.
   c) 79.9, 87, 76.
   d) Not enough information given.
   e) None of the above.

7. A shop sells 3 kinds of t-shirts: one design sells for $4.50, the second for $13.25, and the third for $15.50. If the shop sold 8 shirts of the first design, 12 shirts of the second design, and 4 shirts of the third design, what was the average selling price of the shirts?
   a) $10.71.
   b) $10.25.
   c) $14.55.
   d) $12.55.
   e) $5.80.

Test Your Knowledge: Mean, Median, Mode – Answers

1. **d)**
   If test A avg = 21 for 5 tests, then sum of test A results = 21 * 5 = 105.
   If test B avg = 23 for 13 tests, then sum of test B results = 23 * 13 = 299.
   So total result = 299 + 105 = 404.
   Average of all tests = 404/(5 + 13) = 404/18 = 22.44.

2. **b)**
   The average of the first 6 points is 12 → $s_1/6 = 12$ → $s_1 = 72$; s_1 is the sum of the first 6 points.

   The average of the next 2 points is 20 → $s_2/2 = 20$ → $s_2 = 40$; s_2 is the sum of the next 2 points.

   The average of the remaining 4 points is 4 → $s_3/4 = 4$ → $s_3 = 16$; s_3 is the sum of the last 4 points.

   The sum of all the data points = 72 + 40 + 16 = 128.

   The average = 128/12 = 10.67.

3. **e)**
   Average = (3 * 55 + 2 * 35 + 3 * 70)/8 → Average = 55.625.

4. **c)**
   Average of high s = (80 + 95 + 78 + 79 + 94 + 67 + 76)/7 = 81.29.

   Average of low s = (45 + 34 + 47 + 55 + 35 + 46 + 54)/7 = 45.14.

5. **c)**
   To find the median, we first have to put the list in order:

   27, 28, 29, 30, 35, 37, 41, 43, 44, 45, 46, 50.

   The middle two scores are 37 and 41, and their average is 39.

6. **e) None of the above**
   The mean is just the total score/number of scores → 90 +... + 94)/10 → 79.9.

   The median is the score located in the middle. The middle of the set of the numbers is between 84 and 79. The average of these two scores is 81.5.

   The mode is the number that occurs the most: 78.

7. **a)**
   Multiply each t-shirt price with the number sold; add them together and divide by the total number of shirts sold.

   So Average Price = (4.50 * 8 + 13.25 * 12 + 15.50 * 4)/(8 + 12 + 4) → $10.71.

Test Your Knowledge: Exponents and Roots

1. What is $x^2y^3z^5/y^2z^{-9}$?
   a) y^5z^4.
   b) yz^4.
   c) x^2yz^{14}.
   d) $x^2y^5z^4$.
   e) xyz.

2. What is k if $(2m^3)^5 = 32m^{k+1}$?
   a) 11.
   b) 12.
   c) 13.
   d) 14.
   e) 15.

3. What is $x^5y^4z^3/x^{-3}y^2z^{-4}$?
   a) $x^6y^4z^7$.
   b) x^8yz^7.
   c) x^6yz^7.
   d) $x^8y^2z^7$.
   e) $x^6y^2z^7$.

4. Evaluate $(a^2 * a^{54} + a^{56} + (a^{58}/a^2))/a^4$.
   a) a^{56}.
   b) $3a^{56}$.
   c) $3a^{52}$.
   d) $3a^{54}$.
   e) a^{54}.

5. $9^m = 3^{-1/n}$. What is mn?
   a) .5.
   b) 2.
   c) -2.
   d) -.5.
   e) -1.

6. If $2^a * 4^a = 32$, what is a?
   a) 1/3.
   b) 2/3.
   c) 1.
   d) 4/3.
   e) 5/3.

2. d)
Expand $(2ar^3)^5$ to give $32m^{15}$.

So $32m^{15} = 32m^{k+1} \rightarrow k+1 = 15 \rightarrow k = 14.$

3. d)
$$x^5y^4z^3/x^{-3}y^2z^{-4} = x^5y^4z^3 * x^3y^{-2}z^4 = x^8y^2z^7.$$

4. c)
$$(a^2*a^{54}+a^{56}+ (a^{58}/a^2))/a^4 = (a^{54}+2+a^{56}+a^{58}-2)a^{-4} = 3a^{56}-4 = 3a^{52}.$$

5. d)
9^m is the same as 3^{2m}.

So $3^{2m} = 3^{-1/n} \rightarrow 2m = -1/n \rightarrow mn = -.5.$

6. e)
$2^a * 4^a$ can be re-written as $2^a * (2^2)^a$.

$32 = 2^5$.

Therefore, $2^{(a+2a)} = 2^5 \rightarrow 3a = 5 \rightarrow a = 5/3.$

Test Your Knowledge: Algebraic Equations

1. The number $568cd$ should be divisible by 2, 5, and 7. What are the values of the digits c and d?
    a) 56835.
    b) 56830.
    c) 56860.
    d) 56840.
    e) 56800.

2. Carla is 3 times older than her sister Megan. Eight years ago, Carla was 18 years older than her sister. What is Megan's age?
    a) 10.
    b) 8.
    c) 9.
    d) 6.
    e) 5.

3. What is the value of $f(x) = (x^2 - 25)/(x + 5)$ when $x = 0$?
    a) -1.
    b) -2.
    c) -3.
    d) -4.
    e) -5.

4. Four years from now, John will be twice as old as Sally will be. If Sally was 10 eight years ago, how old is John?
    a) 35.
    b) 40.
    c) 45.
    d) 50.
    e) 55.

5. I have some marbles. I give 25% to Vic, 20% to Robbie, 10% to Jules. I then give 6/20 of the remaining amount to my brother, and keep the rest for myself. If I end up with 315 marbles, how many did I have to begin with?
    a) 1000.
    b) 1500.
    c) 3500.
    d) 400.
    e) 500.

6. I have some marbles. I give 25% to Vic, 20% of the remainder to Robbie, 10% of that remainder to Jules and myself I then give 6/20 of the remaining amount to my brother, and keep the rest for myself. If I end up with 315 marbles, how many did I have to begin with?
    a) 800.
    b) 833.
    c) 834.
    d) 378.
    e) 500.

8. A bag of marbles has 8 marbles. If I buy 2 bags of marbles, how many
   need to buy to have a total of at least 45 marbles?

   a) 3.
   b) 4.
   c) 5.
   d) 6.
   e) 29.

9. A factory that produces widgets wants to sell them each for $550. It costs $50 for the raw materials
   for each widget, and the startup cost for the factory was $10000. How many widgets have to be sold
   so that the factory can break even?

   a) 10.
   b) 20.
   c) 30.
   d) 40.
   e) 50.

10. Expand $(3x - 4)(6 - 2x)$.
    a) $6x^2 - 6x + 8$.
    b) $-6x^2 + 26x - 24$.
    c) $6x^2 - 26x + 24$.
    d) $-6x^2 + 26x + 24$.
    e) $6x^2 + 26x - 24$.

11. If $6n + m$ is divisible by 3 and 5, which of the following numbers when added to $6n + m$ will still give
    a result that is divisible by 3 and 5?

    a) 4.
    b) 6.
    c) 12.
    d) 20.
    e) 60.

12. If x is negative, and $x^3/5$ and $x/5$ both give the same result, what could be the value of x?
    a) -5.
    b) -4.
    c) 3.
    d) 0.
    e) -1.

13. If $m = 3548$, and $n = 235$, then what is the value of $m * n$?
   a) 87940.
   b) 843499.
   c) 87900.
   d) 8830.
   e) 833780.

14. A ball is thrown at a speed of 30 mph. How far will it travel in 2 minutes and 35 seconds?
   a) 1.5 miles.
   b) 1.20 miles.
   c) 1.29 miles.
   d) 1.3 miles.
   e) 1.1 miles.

15. Simplify: $30(\sqrt{40} - \sqrt{60})$.
   a) $30(\sqrt{5} - \sqrt{15})$.
   b) $30(\sqrt{10} + \sqrt{15})$.
   c) $60(\sqrt{5} + \sqrt{15})$.
   d) $60(\sqrt{10} - \sqrt{15})$.
   e) 60.

16. Simplify: $30/(\sqrt{40} - \sqrt{60})$.
   a) $3(\sqrt{5} + \sqrt{15})$.
   b) $-3(\sqrt{5} - \sqrt{15})$.
   c) $-3(\sqrt{10} + \sqrt{15})$.
   d) $3(\sqrt{10} + \sqrt{15})$.
   e) $3(\sqrt{10} - \sqrt{15})$.

17. What is the least common multiple of 2, 3, 4, and 5?
   a) 30.
   b) 60.
   c) 120.
   d) 40.
   e) 50.

18. It costs $6 to make a pen that sells for $12. How many pens need to be sold to make a profit of $60?
   a) 10.
   b) 6.
   c) 72.
   d) 30.
   e) 12.

Test Your Knowledge: Algebraic Equations - Answers

1. **d)**

   If the number is divisible by 2, d should be even. If the number is divisible by 5, then b has ~~?~~
   0.

   Start by making both variables 0 and dividing by the largest factor, 7.

   $56800/7 = 8114$.

   2 from 56800 is 56798, a number divisible by 2 and 7.

   Next add a multiple of 7 that turns the last number to a 0. $6 * 7 = 42$. $56798 + 42 = 56840$, which is divisible by 2, 5, and 7.

2. **c)**

   Carla's age is c; Megan's age is m. $c = 3m$; $c - 8 = m - 8 + 18$.

   Substitute $3m$ for c in equation 2 → $3m - 8 = m + 10$ → $m = 9$.

3. **e)**

   We know $(x^2 - 25) = (x + 5)(x - 5)$.

   So $(x^2 - 25)/(x + 5) = x - 5$. At $x = 0$, $f(0) = -5$.

4. **b)**

   Let j be John's age and s be Sally's age.

   $j + 4 = 2(s + 4)$.

   $s - 8 = 10$ → $s = 18$.

   So $j + 4 = 2(18 + 4)$ → $j = 40$.

5. **a)**

   If x is the number of marbles initially, then $.25x$ goes to Vic, $.2x$ goes to Robbie, and $.1x$ goes to Jules.

   The number left, x, is $(1 - .25 - .2 - .1) = .45x$.

   Of that I give 6/20 to my brother, so $6/20 * .45x$.

   I am left with $.45x(1 - (6/20)) = .315x$.

   We are also told $.315x = 315$ → $x = 1000$.

6. **c)**

Always read the question carefully! Questions 5 and 6 are similar, but they are not the same.

Let x be the original number of marbles. After Vic's share is given .75x remains. After Robbie's share .75x * .80 remains. After Jules' share, .75x * .8 * .9 remains.

After I give my brother his share, .75x * .8 * .9 * (1 - 6/20) remains. The remaining number = .378x.

We are told .378x = 315 → x = 833.33. We need to increase this to the next highest number, 834, because we have part of a marble and to include it we need to have a whole marble.

7. **c)**

Replace the value of x with its value and solve the equation.

$29 = 5y + 4$.

Solving:

$29 - 4 = 5y + 4 - 4$.

$25 = 5y$ or $5y = 25$.

$5y/5 = 25/5$.

$y = 5$.

8. **b)**

$2(8) + x > 45$ means $x > 29$, so we need more than 29 marbles. A bag has 8 marbles, so the number of bags needed is 29/8, or 3.625. Since we need 3 bags + part of another bag, we need 4 additional bags to give at least 45 marbles.

9. **b)**

n is the number of widgets. The cost the factory incurs for making n widgets is $10000 + 50n$. The amount the factory makes by selling n widgets is $550n$.

At the break-even point, the cost incurred is equal to the amount of sales.

$10000 + 50n = 550n$ → $n = 20$.

10. **b)**

Use FOIL:

$(3x - 4)(6 - 2x) = 3x * 6 - 4 * 6 + 3x * (-2x) - 4 * (-2x) = 18x - 24 - 6x^2 + 8x = -6x^2 + 26x - 24$.

11. **e)**

Since $6n + m$ is divisible by 3 and 5, the new number that we get after adding a value will be divisible by 3 and 5 only if the value that we add is divisible by 3 and 5. The only number that will work from the given choices is 60.

12. e)

We are told $x^3/5 = x/5 \rightarrow x^3 = x$. The possible values are -1, 0, and 1. We are told that x is negative.

So $x = -1$.

13. e)

This problem can be done by elimination. We know that m is in the thousands, which means $x * 10^3$; and n is in the hundreds, which is $y * 10^2$. The answer will be $z * 10^5$, or 6 places in total, so we can eliminate **a)**, **c)**, and **d)**. Also we see that m ends in 8 and n ends in 5, so the answer has to end in 0 ($8 * 5 = 40$), which eliminates **b)**.

14. c)

The ball has a speed of 30 miles per hour. 30 miles per 60 minutes = .5 mile per minute; 2 minutes and 35 seconds = 2 minutes; and 35/60 minutes = 2.58 minutes.

The ball travels .5 * 2.58 = 1.29 miles.

15. d)

$30\left(\sqrt{40} - \sqrt{60}\right) = 30\sqrt{4\,(10 - 15)} = 60\left(\sqrt{10} - \sqrt{15}\right).$

16. c)

Multiply the numerator and the denominator by $\left(\sqrt{40} + \sqrt{60}\right)$.

So $\dfrac{30}{\left(\sqrt{40}-\sqrt{60}\right)} * \left[\dfrac{\left(\sqrt{40}+\sqrt{60}\right)}{\left(\sqrt{40}+\sqrt{60}\right)}\right] = $
$30\left(\sqrt{40} + \sqrt{60}\right)/\left(\sqrt{40} - \sqrt{60}\right)^2.$

$-3\left(\sqrt{10} + \sqrt{15}\right).$

17. b)

Find all the prime numbers that multiply to give the numbers.

For 2, prime factor is 2; for 3, prime factor is 3; for 4, prime factors are 2, 2; and for 5, prime factor is 5. Note the maximum times of occurrence of each prime and multiply these to find the least common multiple.

The LCM is 2 * 2 * 3 * 5 = 60.

18. a)

One pen sells for $12, so on the sale of a pen, the profit is 12 - 6 = 6.

In order to make $60, we need to sell 10 pens.

Test Your Knowledge: Inequalities, Literal Equations, Polynomials, and Binomials

1. If $x < 5$ and $y < 6$, then $x + y$ __?__ 11.
   a) $<$
   b) $>$
   c) $\leq$
   d) $\geq$
   e) $=$

2. Which of the following is true about the inequality $25x^2 - 40x - 32 < 22$?
   a) There are no solutions.
   b) There is a set of solutions.
   c) There is 1 solution only.
   d) There are 2 solutions.
   e) There are 3 solutions.

3. If $x - 2y > 6$, what possible values of y always have x as greater than or equal to 2?
   a) $y \geq 1$.
   b) $y \leq 0$.
   c) $y \geq -2$.
   d) $y < 2$.
   e) $y \leq 6$.

4. Find the point of intersection of the lines $x + 2y = 4$ and $3x - y = 26$.
   a) $(1, 3)$.
   b) $(8, -2)$.
   c) $(0, 2)$.
   d) $(2, -1)$.
   e) $(4, 26)$.

5. If $a + b = 2$, and $a - b = 4$, what is a?
   a) 1.
   b) 2.
   c) 3.
   d) 4.
   e) 5.

6. If $\sqrt{a} + \sqrt{b} = 2$, and $\sqrt{a} - \sqrt{b} = 3$, what is $a + b$?
   a) 6.5.
   b) 6.
   c) 5.5.
   d) 5.
   e) 4.5.

7. If $a = b + 3$, and $3b = 5a + 6$, what is $3a - 2b$?
   - a) -1.5.
   - b) 2.5.
   - c) 3.
   - d) 4.3.
   - e) 5.

8. The sum of the roots of a quadratic equation is 8, and the difference is 2. What is the equation?
   - a) $x^2 - 8x - 15$.
   - b) $x^2 + 8x + 15$.
   - c) $x^2 - 8x + 15$.
   - d) $x^2 + 8x - 15$.
   - e) $x^2 + 15$.

9. Solve the following system of equations: $3x + 2y = 7$ and $3x + y = 5$.
   - a) $x = 2, y = 1$.
   - b) $x = 2, y = 2$.
   - c) $x = 1, y = 0$.
   - d) $x = 1, y = 2$.
   - e) $x = 1, y = 1$.

10. Nine tickets were sold for $41. If the tickets cost $4 and $5, how many $5 tickets were sold?
    - a) 5.
    - b) 4.
    - c) 9.
    - d) 6.
    - e) 7.

11. Joe brought a bag of 140 M&Ms to his class of 40 students. Each boy received 2 M&Ms. Each girl received 4. How many boys were in the class?
    - a) 10.
    - b) 20.
    - c) 30.
    - d) 40.
    - e) 50.

Test Your Knowledge: Inequalities, Literal Equations, Polynomials, and Binomials – Answers

1. **a)**

   Choice **a)** will always be true, while the other choices can never be true.

2. **b)**

   $25x^2 - 40x + 32 < 22 \rightarrow 25x^2 - 40x + 16 < 6 \rightarrow (5x - 4)^2 < 6 \rightarrow 5x - 4 < 6.$

   $x = 2$, so x has to be all numbers less than 2 for this inequality to work.

3. **c)**

   Rearrange equation $x > 6 + 2y$, so $2 > 6 + 2y$. Solve for y.

   $2 \geq 6 + 2y.$

   $-4 \geq 2y$, so $-2 \leq y$ or $y \geq -2$.

   (When working with inequalities, remember to reverse the sign when dividing by a negative number.)

4. **b)**

   Find the slopes first. If they are not equal, then the lines intersect. The slopes are -1/2 and 3.

   Next, solve by substitution or addition. From the first equation, $x = 4 - 2y$. Plugging this into equation 2, we get $3(4 - 2y) - y = 26 \rightarrow 7y = 12 - 26 \rightarrow y = -2$. Plug this value into either equation to find x.

   With equation 1, we get $x - 4 = 4 \rightarrow x = 8$.

5. **c)**

   Add the equations to eliminate b. $2a = 6 \rightarrow a = 3$.

6. **a)**

   Square both equations.

   Equation 1 becomes $a + 2\sqrt{ab} + b = 4$; and equation 2 becomes $a - 2\sqrt{ab} + b = 9$.

   Add the equations. $2(a + b) = 13 \rightarrow a + b = 13/2$. $13/2 = 6.5$.

7. **a)**

   Solve by substitution.

   If $a = b + 3$, and $3b = 5a + 6$, then $3b = 5(b+3) + 6$.

   If $3b - 5b - 15 = 6$, then $-2b = 21$. Therefore, $b = -10.5$.

   Now use substitution to find a. $a = b + 3$. So $a = -10.5 + 3$. Therefore, $a = -7.5$.

   Solve the equation, $3a - 2b$. $3(-7.5) - 2(-10.5) = -1.5$.

8. c)

If the roots are a and b, then $a + b = 8$ and $a - b = 2$.

Add the equations. $2a = 10 \rightarrow a = 5 \rightarrow b = 3$.

The factors are $(x - 5)(x - 3)$, and the equation is $x^2 - 8x + 15$.

9. d)

From the equation $3x + y = 5$, we get $y = 5 - 3x$. Substitute into the other equation. $3x + 2(5 - 3x) = 7 \rightarrow 3x + 10 - 6x = 7 \rightarrow x = 1$. This value into either of the equations gives us $y = 2$.

10. a)

$4x + 5y = 41$, and $x + y = 9$, where x and y are the number of tickets sold.

From equation 2: $x = 9 - y$.

From equation 1: $4(9 - y) + 5y = 41 \rightarrow 36 + y = 41 \rightarrow y = 5$.

11. a)

b is the number of boys, and g is the number of girls. So $b + g = 40$, and $2b + 4g = 140$.

To do the problem, use the substitution method. Plug $(g = 40 - b)$ into $(2b + 4g = 140)$.

$2b + 4(40 - b) = 140 \rightarrow b = 10$.

Test Your Knowledge: Slope and Distance to Midpoint

1. What is the equation of the line that passes through (3, 5), with intercept $y = 8$?
    a) $y = x + 8$.
    b) $y = x - 8$.
    c) $y = -x - 8$.
    d) $y = -x + 8$.
    e) $y = -x$.

2. What is the value of y in the equation $(3x - 4)^2 = 4y - 15$, if $x = 3$?
    a) 10.
    b) 2.5.
    c) -10.
    d) -2.5.
    e) 5.

3. If $y = 4x + 6y$, what is the range of y if $-10 < x \leq 5$?
    a) $-4 < y \leq 8$.
    b) $-4 < y < 8$.
    c) $8 > y > -4$.
    d) $-4 \leq y < 8$.
    e) $-4 \leq y \leq 8$.

4. If Jennifer gets three times as much allowance as Judy gets, and Judy gets $5/week, how much does Jennifer get every month?
    a) $15.
    b) $20.
    c) $30.
    d) $45.
    e) $60.

5. What is the value of x, if $y = 8$ in the equation $5x + 9y = 3x - 6y + 5$?
    a) 57.5.
    b) 60.
    c) -60.
    d) -57.5.
    e) None of the above.

6.

A (3, 5)   B (8, 17)

What is the area outside the circle, but within the square whose two corners are A and B?
   a) 169(1-π).
   b) 169 π.
   c) 169 π /4.
   d) 169(1- π /4).
   e) 169.

7. A line with a slope of 2 passes through the point (2, 4). What is the set of coordinates where that line passes through the y intercept?
   a) (-2, 0).
   b) (0, 0).
   c) (2, 2).
   d) (4, 0).
   e) (1, 1).

8.

$$3x + 4y = 7$$
$$9x + 12y = 21$$

Determine where the above two lines intersect:
   a) $x = 4, y = 3$.
   b) $x = 12, y = 9$.
   c) $x = 1/3, y = 1/3$.
   d) Not enough information provided.
   e) There is no solution; the lines do not intersect.

9.

$$3x + 4y = 7$$
$$8x - 6y = 9$$

Are the above lines parallel or perpendicular?
   a) Parallel.
   b) Perpendicular.
   c) Neither parallel nor perpendicular.
   d) Cannot be determined.
   e) The angle at the point of intersection is 40.

10. Is the graph of the function $f(x) = -3x^2 + 4$ linear, asymptotical, symmetrical to the x axis, symmetrical to the y axis, or not symmetrical to either axis?

    a) Symmetrical to the x axis.
    b) Symmetrical to the y axis.
    c) Symmetrical to neither axis.
    d) Asymptotic.
    e) Linear.

11. Two points on a line have coordinates (3, 12) and (9, 20). What is the distance between these two points?

    a) 10.
    b) 12.
    c) 13.
    d) 8.
    e) 11.

12. In the following graph, what is the equation of line AB if line AB is perpendicular to line PQ? Point coordinates are:

M (-4, 0); O (0, 2); and N (0, -3). The lines intersect at (-2,1).

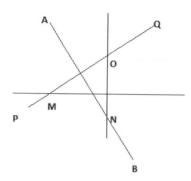

    a) $y = 2x + 3$.
    b) $y = -2x - 3$.
    c) $y = x - 4$.
    d) $y = x + 3$.
    e) $y = -2x - 3$.

13. What is the equation of a line passing through (1, 2) and (6, 12)?

    a) $y = x$.
    b) $y = 2x$.
    c) $y = x/2$.
    d) $y = 2x + 2$.
    e) $y = x - 2$.

14. What is the midpoint of the line connecting points (0, 8) and (2, 6)?

    a) (-1, 1).
    b) (2, 14).
    c) (-2, 2).
    d) (0, 1).
    e) (1, 7).

15. What is the equation of a line passing through $(1, 1)$ and $(2, 4)$?

    a) $3y = x + 2$.
    b) $2y = x + 3$.
    c) $y = 3x - 2$.
    d) $4x = y + 2$.
    e) $y = (1/3)x + 2$.

16. Line A passes through $(0, 0)$ and $(3, 4)$. Line B passes through $(2, 6)$ and $(3, y)$. What value of y will make the lines parallel?

    a) 20/3.
    b) 7.
    c) 22/3.
    d) 29.
    e) 5.

17. Line A passes through $(1, 3)$ and $(3, 4)$. Line B passes through $(3, 7)$ and $(5, y)$. What value of y will make the lines perpendicular?

    a) 1.
    b) 2.
    c) 3.
    d) 4.
    e) 5.

18. What is the equation of line A that is perpendicular to line B, connecting $(8, 1)$ and $(10, 5)$, that intersects at $(x, 14)$?

    a) $y = 2x - 7$.
    b) $y = -2x + 7$.
    c) $y = (-1/2)x + 19\frac{1}{4}$.
    d) $y = 5x - 7$.
    e) $y = 2x - 19\frac{1}{4}$.

Test Your Knowledge: Slope and Distance to Midpoint – Answers

1. **d)**

   The standard form of the line equation is $y = mx + b$. We need to find slope m.

   $m = (y_2 - y_1)/(x_2 - x_1)$ → $m = (5 - 8)/(3 - 0)$ → $m = -1$.

   Therefore the equation is $y = -x + 8$.

2. **a)**

   At $x = 3$, $((3 * 3) - 4)^2 = 4y - 15$.

   $(9 - 4)^2 = 4y - 15$.

   $25 = 4y - 15$.

   $40 = 4y$.

   $y = 10$.

3. **d)**

   Rearrange the equation and combine like terms. $-5y = 4x$.

   At $x = -10$, $y = 8$. At $x = 5$, $y = -4$. The range of y is therefore $-4 \le y < 8$.

4. **e)**

   If Judy gets x dollars, then Jennifer gets $3x$ in a week. In a month, Jennifer will then get $4 * 3x$.

   If Judy gets $5 per week, then Jennifer gets $60 in a month.

5. **d)**

   Combine like terms.

   $5x + 9y = 3x - 6y + 5$ → $2x = -15y + 5$ → $x = -57.5$ when $y = 8$.

6. **d)**

   First we need to find the length of side AB.

   $AB = \sqrt{(17 - 5)^2 + (8 - 3)^2} = 13$.

   If $AB = 13$, then $A_{square} = 13^2 = 169$.

   AB is also the diameter of the circle. $A_{circle} \pi (d^2/4) = 169 \pi /4$.

   The area outside the circle and within the square is: $A_{square} - A_{circle} = 169(1 - \pi /4)$.

7. b)

The slope of the line is given as $m = (y_2 - y_1)/(x_2 - x_1)$, where (x_1, y_1) and (x_2, y_2) are two points which the line passes through.

The y intercept is the point where the graph intersects the y axis, so $x = 0$ at this point.

Plug in the values of m, etc.; we get $2 = (4 - y)/(2 - 0)$ → $y = 0$.

8. e)

While it is tempting to solve this system of simultaneous equations to find the values of x and y, the first thing to do is to see whether the lines intersect. To do this, compare the slopes of the two lines by putting the lines into the standard form, $y = mx + b$, where m is the slope.

By rearranging, equation 1 becomes $y = 7/4 - 3x/4$; and equation 2 becomes $y = 21/12 - 9x/12$.

The slope of line 1 is -3/4, and the slope of line 2 is -9/12, which reduces to -3/4. Since the slopes are equal, the lines are parallel and do not intersect.

9. b)

Find the slopes by rearranging the two equations into the form $y = mx + b$.

Equation 1 becomes $y = -3x/4 + 7/4$ and equation 2 becomes $y = 8x/6 - 9/6$.

So $m_1 = -3/4$ and $m_2 = 8/6 = 4/3$. We see that m_1 is the negative inverse of m_2, so line 1 is perpendicular to line 2.

10. b)

Find the values of the y coordinate for different values of the x coordinate (example, [-3, +3]). We get the following chart:

x	y
-3	-23
-2	-8
-1	1
0	4
1	1
2	-8
3	-23

From these values, we see the graph is symmetrical to the y axis.

11. a)

Distance $s = \sqrt{(x_2 - x_1)^2 + (y_2 - y_1)^2}$ → $s = \sqrt{(9 - 3)^2 + (20 - 12)^2} = \sqrt{36 + 64} = 10$.

12. b)

$y = mx + b$; m is the slope and b is the y intercept.

Calculate m for line AB using the given points (0, -3) and (-2, 1). $m = (-3 - 1)/(0 - (-2)) = -2$. The y intercept is -3 (from point set given), so $y = -2x - 3$.

51

13. b)

First, find the slope, $(y_2-y_1)/(x_2-x_1)$ → slope = $(12 - 2)/(6 - 1) = 2$.

Next, use the slope and a point to find the value of b.

In the standard line equation, $y = mx + b$, use the point $(6, 12)$ to get $12 = (2 * 6) + b$ → $b = 0$.

The equation of the line is $y = 2x$.

14. e)

The midpoint is at $(x_1 + x_2)/2, (y_1 + y_2)/2 = (1,7)$.

15. c)

Slope $= (y_2 - y_1)/(x_2 - x_1) = 3$. Plug one of the coordinates into $y = mx + b$ to find the value of b.

$1 = 3(1) + b$ → $b = -2$.

The equation of the line is $y = 3x - 2$.

16. c)

Calculate the slope of each line. Slope of line A = 4/3; and slope of line B = $y - 6$.

The slopes of the line have to be the same for the lines to be parallel.

$4/3 = y - 6$ → $4 = 3y - 18$ → $y = 22/3$.

17. c)

The slope of line A = ½; and the slope of line B = $(y - 7)/2$.

The product of the slopes has to equal -1.

$(1/2)[(y - 7)/2] = -1$ → $(y - 7)/4 = -1$ → $y = 3$.

18. c)

$Slope_b = (5 - 1)/(10 - 8) = 2$. The slope of line A is -1/2.

To find the intercept of line B, use $y = mx + b$.

$5 = (2)(10) + b$, so $b = -7$. Equation of line B is $y = 2x - 7$.

Find intersect x, using the given y coordinate. $14 = 2x - 7; x = 10.5$.

Find the intercept of line A using the coordinates of intersection.

$14 = (-1/2)(10.5)+b$. $b = 19\frac{1}{4}$.

The equation of line A is $y = -(1/2)x + 19\frac{1}{4}$.

Test Your Knowledge: Absolute Value Equations

1. Factor $x^2 + 2x - 15$.
   a) $(x - 3)(x + 5)$.
   b) $(x + 3)(x - 5)$.
   c) $(x + 3)(x + 5)$.
   d) $(x - 3)(x - 5)$.
   e) $(x - 1)(x + 15)$.

2. Car A starts at 3:15 PM and travels straight to its destination at a constant speed of 50 mph. If it arrives at 4:45 PM, how far did it travel?
   a) 70 miles.
   b) 75 miles.
   c) 65 miles.
   d) 40 miles.
   e) 105 miles.

3. What are the roots of the equation $2x^2 + 14x = 0$?
   a) 0 and 7.
   b) 0 and -7.
   c) 14 and 0.
   d) 2 and 14.
   e) Cannot be determined.

4. If $f(x) = 2x^2 + 3x$, and $g(x) = x + 4$, what is $f[g(x)]$?
   a) $x^2 + 19x + 44$.
   b) $2x^2 + 19x + 44$.
   c) $4x^2 + 35x + 76$.
   d) $x^2 + 8x + 16$.
   e) None of the above.

5. If $|x + 4| = 2$, what are the values of x?
   a) 2 and 6.
   b) -2 and -6.
   c) -2.
   d) -6.
   e) 0.

6. The sale of an item can be written as a function of price: $s = 3p + c$, where s is the amount in sales, p is the price per item, and c is a constant value. If the sales generated are $20 at a price of $5 for the item, then what should the price be to generate $50 in sales?
   a) $10.
   b) $15.
   c) $20.
   d) $16.
   e) $14.

7. If $f(n) = 2n + 3\sqrt{n}$, where n is a positive integer, what is $f[g(5)]$ if $g(m) = m - 4$?
    a) 1.
    b) 2.
    c) 3.
    d) 4.
    e) 5.

8. If $f(x) = (x + 2)^2$, and $-4 \leq x \leq 4$, what is the minimum value of $f(x)$?
    a) 0.
    b) 1.
    c) 2.
    d) 3.
    e) 4.

9. If $f(x) = (x + 2)^2$, and $0 \leq x \leq 4$, what is the minimum value of $f(x)$?
    a) 1.
    b) 2.
    c) 3.
    d) 4.
    e) 5.

10. What is $x^2 - 9$ divided by $x - 3$?
    a) $x - 3$.
    b) $x + 3$.
    c) x.
    d) $x - 1$.
    e) 6.

11. An equation has two roots: 5 and -8. What is a possible equation?
    a) $x^2 - 3x + 40$.
    b) $x^2 - 3x - 40$.
    c) $x^2 + x + 40$.
    d) $x^2 + 3x - 40$.
    e) $2x^2 - 3x + 40$.

12. In an ant farm, the number of ants grows every week according to the formula
$N = 100 + 2^w$, where w is the number of weeks elapsed. How many ants will the colony have after 5 weeks?
    a) 115.
    b) 125.
    c) 135.
    d) 132.
    e) 233.

13. Find the values of x that validate the following equation: $[(4x + 5)^2 - (40x + 25)]^{1/2} + 3|x| - 14 = 0$.

a) -2, -14.
b) 2, -14.
c) -2, 14.
d) 2, 14.
e) No solution.

14. If $|x| = 4$ and $|y| = 5$, what are the values of $|x + y|$?

a) 1, 9.
b) -1, 9.
c) -1, -9.
d) -1, -9.
e) $1 < |x + y| < 9$.

15. If $y = |x|$, what is the range of y?

a) $y < 0$.
b) $0 < y < x$.
c) $y > 0$.
d) $y \geq 0$.
e) $y > x$.

Test Your Knowledge: Absolute Value Equations – Answers

1. a)

The constant term is -15. The factors should multiply to give -15 and add to give 2. The numbers -3 and 5 satisfy both, $(x - 3)(x + 5)$.

2. b)

The time between 3:15 PM and 4:45 PM = 1.5 hours. $1.5 * 50 = 75$.

Reminder: half an hour is written as .5 of an hour, not .3 of an hour, even though on a clock a half hour is 30 minutes.

3. b)

Rearrange, reduce, and factor.

$2x^2 + 14x + 0 = 0$.

$2(x^2 + 7x + 0) = 0$.

$(x + 7) (x + 0)$.

$x = 0$, or -7.

4. b)

Substitute $g(x)$ for every x in $f(x)$.

$f[g((x + 4))] = 2(x + 4)^2 + 3(x + 4) = 2x^2 + 16x + 32 + 3x + 12 = 2x^2 + 19x + 44$.

5. b)

Two solutions: $(x + 4) = 2$ and $-(x + 4) = 2$.

Or $x + 4 = 2$, $x = -2$.

And $x + 4 = -2$, $x = -6$.

6. b)

Find the value of the constant by plugging in the given information.

$20 = 3 * 5 + c \rightarrow c = 5$.

Now use the value of c and the new value of s to find $p. 50 = 3p + 5 \rightarrow p = 15$.

7. e)

$g(5) = 5 - 4 = 1. f[g(5)] = 2 * 1 + 3\sqrt{1} = 5$.

8. a)

From the domain of x, the lowest value of x is -4, and the highest value is 4. We are tempted to think that $f(x)$ will have the least value at $x = -4$: $f(-4) = 4$. However, $f(x)$ is equal to a squared value, so the lowest value of $f(x)$ is 0. This happens at $x = -2$.

9. d)

The lowest value of $f(x)$ can be 0, since $f(x)$ is equal to a squared value, but, for $f(x) = 0$, x must equal -2. That is outside the domain of x. The least value of $f(x) = 4$.

10. b)

$x^2 - 9$ can be factored into $(x + 3)$ and $(x - 3)$.

$[(x + 3)(x - 3)]/(x - 3) = x + 3$.

11. d)

If the roots are 5 and -8, then the factors are $(x - 5)(x + 8)$. Multiply the factors to get the equation.

$x^2 + 3x - 40$.

12. d)

After 5 weeks, the number of ants $= 100 + 32$, or 132.

13. d)

Expand the equation:

$[16x^2 + 40x + 25 - 40x - 25]^{1/2} + 3|x| - 14 = 0$.

$(16x^2)^{1/2} + 3|x| - 14 = 0$.

$4x + 3|x| - 14 = 0$.

$3|x| = 14 - 4x$.

$|x| = \dfrac{14}{3} - \dfrac{4x}{3}$ $\qquad x = \dfrac{14}{3} - \dfrac{4x}{3} = 2$ $\qquad x = -\dfrac{14}{3} - \dfrac{4x}{3} = 14$.

14. a)

$x = 4$ and $y = 5$, $|x + y| = 9$.

$x = -4$ and $y = 5$, $|x + y| = 1$.

$x = 4$ and $y = -5$, $|x + y| = 1$.

$x = -4$ and $y = -5$, $|x + y| = 9$.

15. d)

The absolute value of x can be at least a 0, and is otherwise positive regardless of the value of x.

$y \geq 0$.

Test Your Knowledge: Geometry

1. What is the area, in square feet, of the triangle whose sides have lengths equal to 3, 4, and 5 feet?
   a) 6 square feet.
   b) 7 square feet.
   c) 4 square feet.
   d) 5 square feet.
   e) 8 square feet.

2. In the following figure, where AE bisects line BC, and angles AEC and AEB are both right angles, what is the length of AB?
   a) 1 cm.
   b) 2 cm.
   c) 3 cm.
   d) 4 cm.
   e) 5 cm.

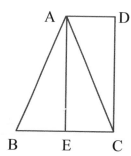

BC = 6 cm
AD = 3 cm
CD = 4 cm

3. In the following triangle, if AB = 6 and BC = 8, what should the length of CA be to make triangle ABC a right triangle?
   a) 10.
   b) 9.
   c) 8.
   d) 4.
   e) 7.

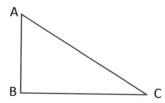

4. In the following circle there is a square with an area of 36 cm². What is the area outside the square, but within the circle?
   a) 18π cm².
   b) $18\pi - 30$ cm².
   c) $18\pi - 36$ cm².
   d) 18 cm².
   e) -18 cm².

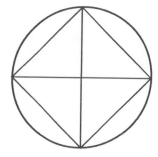

5. The length of a rectangle is 4 times its width. If the width of the rectangle is $5 - x$ inches, and the perimeter of the rectangle is 30 inches, what is x?

    a) 1.
    b) 2.
    c) 3.
    d) 4.
    e) 5.

6. Two sides of a triangle have a ratio AC:BC = 5:4. The length of AB on a similar triangle = 24. What is the actual value of AC for the larger triangle?

    a) 10.
    b) 14.4.
    c) 35.
    d) 40.
    e) 50.

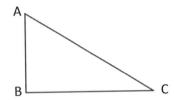

7. If the diameter of a circle is doubled, the area increases by what factor?

    a) 1 time.
    b) 2 times.
    c) 3 times.
    d) 4 times.
    e) 5 times.

8. In the following triangle PQR, what is the measure of angle A?

    a) 145^0.
    b) 140^0.
    c) 70^0.
    d) 50^0.
    e) 40^0.

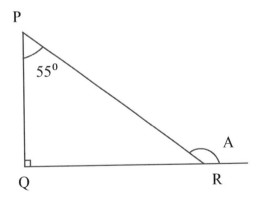

Test Your Knowledge: Geometry – Answers

1. **a)**

   The Pythagorean triple (special right triangle property) means the two shorter sides form a right triangle.

   $1/2 bh$ = A. So, $(1/2)(3)(4) = 6$.

2. **e)**

   $AB^2 = AC^2 = AD2 + CD^2 \rightarrow AB^2 = 3^2 + 4^2 \rightarrow AB = 5$.

3. **a)**

   In a right triangle, the square of the hypotenuse = the sum of the squares of the other two sides.

   $AB^2 + BC^2 = AC^2 \rightarrow AC^2 = 36 + 64 \rightarrow AC = 10$.

4. **c)**

   If the area of the square is 36 cm^2, then each side is 6 cm. If we look at the triangle made by half the square, that diagonal would be the hypotenuse of the triangle, and its length = $\sqrt{6^2 + 6^2} = 6\sqrt{2}$.

   This hypotenuse is also the diameter of the circle, so the radius of the circle is $3\sqrt{2}$.

   The area of the circle = $A = \pi r^2 = 18\pi$.

   The area outside the square, but within the circle is $18\pi - 36$.

5. **b)**

   Perimeter of a rectangle = $2(l + w)$. Width = $5 - x$; and length = $4(5 - x)$.

   Perimeter = $2(l * w) = 30 \rightarrow 2(20 - 4x + 5 - x) = 30 \rightarrow -10x = -20 \rightarrow x = 2$.

6. **d)**

   Side AC = 5, and side BC = 4. The Pythagorean triple is 3:4:5, so side AB = 3.

   Because the other triangle is similar, the ratio of all sides is constant. AB:AB = 3:24. The ratio factor is 8.

   AC of the larger triangle = $5 * 8 = 40$.

7. **d)**

   The area of a circle = πr^2.

   If the diameter is doubled, then the radius is also doubled.

   The new area = $\pi * (2r)^2 = 4 * \pi * r^2$. The area increases four times.

8. **a)**

   $\angle P = 55^0$. $\angle Q = 90^0$. $\angle R = 180 - (55 + 90) = 35^0$, and $\angle A = 180 - 35 = 145^0$.

60

Test Your Knowledge: Fundamental Counting Principle, Permutations, Combinations

1. The wardrobe of a studio contains 4 hats, 3 suits, 5 shirts, 2 pants, and 3 pairs of shoes. How many different ways can these items be put together?
   a) 60.
   b) 300.
   c) 360.
   d) 420.
   e) 500.

2. For lunch, you have a choice between chicken fingers or cheese sticks for an appetizer; turkey, chicken, or veal for the main course; cake or pudding for dessert; and either Coke or Pepsi for a beverage. How many choices of possible meals do you have?
   a) 16.
   b) 24.
   c) 34.
   d) 36.
   e) 8.

3. For an office job, I need to pick 3 candidates out of a pool of 5. How many choices do I have?
   a) 60.
   b) 20.
   c) 10.
   d) 30.
   e) 50.

4. A contractor is supposed to choose 3 tiles out of a stack of 5 tiles to make as many patterns as possible. How many different patterns can he make?
   a) 10.
   b) 20.
   c) 30.
   d) 40.
   e) 60.

5. I have chores to do around the house on a weekend. There are 5 chores I must complete by the end of the day. I can choose to do them in any order, so long as they are all completed. How many choices do I have?
   a) 5.
   b) 25.
   c) 32.
   d) 3125.
   e) 120.

6. Next weekend, I have more chores to do around the house. There are 5 chores I must complete by the end of the day. I can choose to do any 2 of them in any order, and then do any 2 the next day again in any order, and then do the remaining 1 the following day. How many choices do I have?
    a) 20.
    b) 6.
    c) 120.
    d) 130.
    e) 25.

7. A certain lottery play sheet has 10 numbers from which 5 have to be chosen. How many different ways can I pick the numbers?
    a) 150.
    b) 250.
    c) 252.
    d) 143.
    e) 278.

8. At a buffet, there are 3 choices for an appetizer, 6 choices for a beverage, and 3 choices for an entrée. How many different ways can I select food from all the food choices?
    a) 12.
    b) 27.
    c) 36.
    d) 42.
    e) 54.

9. If there is a basket of 10 assorted fruits, and I want to pick out 3 fruits, how many combinations of fruits do I have to choose from?
    a) 130.
    b) 210.
    c) 310.
    d) 120.
    e) 100.

10. How many ways can I pick 3 numbers from a set of 10 numbers?
    a) 720.
    b) 120.
    c) 180.
    d) 150.
    e) 880.

Test Your Knowledge: Fundamental Counting Principle, Permutations, Combinations – Answers

1. **c)**
   The number of ways = 4 * 3 * 5 * 2 * 3 = 360.

2. **b)**
   Multiply the possible number of choices for each item from which you can choose.

   2 * 3 * 2 * 2 = 24.

3. **c)**
   This is a combination problem. The order of the candidates does not matter.

   The number of combinations = 5!/3!(5 - 3)! = 5 * 4/2 * 1 = 10.

4. **e)**
   This is a permutation problem. The order in which the tiles are arranged is counted.

   The number of patterns = 5!/(5 - 3)! = 5 * 4 * 3 = 60.

5. **e)**
   This is a permutation problem. The order in which the chores are completed matters.

   $^5P_5$ = 5!/(5 - 5)! = 5! = 5 * 4 * 3 * 2 * 1 = 120.

6. **c)**
   #Choices$_{today}$ = $^5P_2$ = 5!/(5 - 2)! = 5 * 4 = 20.

   #Choices$_{tomorrow}$ = $^3P_2$ = 3!/1! = 6.

   #Choices$_{day3}$ = 1.

   The total number of permutations = 20 * 6 * 1 = 120.

7. **c)**
   This is a combinations problem. The order of the numbers is not relevant.

   $^{10}n_5$ = 10!/5!(10 - 5)! = 10 * 9 * 8 * 7 * 6/5 * 4 * 3 * 2 * 1 = 252.

8. **e)**
   There are 3 ways to choose an appetizer, 6 ways to choose a beverage, and 3 ways to choose an entrée. The total number of choices = 3 * 6 * 3 = 54.

9. **d)**
   $^{10}C_3$ = 10!/(3!(10 - 3)!) = 10!/(3! * 7!) = 10 * 9 * 8/3 * 2 * 1 = 120.

10. **b)**
    $^{10}P_4$ = 10!/3!(10 - 3)! = 10 * 9 * 8/3 * 2 * 1 = 120.

Test Your Knowledge: Ratios, Proportions, Rate of Change

1. A class has 50% more boys than girls. What is the ratio of boys to girls?
   a) 4:3.
   b) 3:2.
   c) 5:4.
   d) 10:7.
   e) 7:5.

2. A car can travel 30 miles on 4 gallons of gas. If the gas tank has a capacity of 16 gallons, how far can it travel if the tank is ¾ full?
   a) 120 miles.
   b) 90 miles.
   c) 60 miles.
   d) 55 miles.
   e) 65 miles.

3. The profits of a company increase by $5000 every year for five years and then decrease by $2000 for the next two years. What is the average rate of change in the company profit for that seven-year period?
   a) $1000/year.
   b) $2000/year.
   c) $3000/year.
   d) $4000/year.
   e) $5000/year.

4. A bag holds 250 marbles. Of those marbles, 40% are red, 30% are blue, 10% are green, and 20% are black. How many marbles of each color are present in the bag?
   a) Red = 90; Blue = 80; Green = 30; Black = 40.
   b) Red = 80; Blue = 60; Green = 30; Black = 80.
   c) Red = 100; Blue = 75; Green = 25; Black = 50.
   d) Red = 100; Blue = 70; Green = 30; Black = 50.
   e) Red = 120; Blue = 100; Green = 10; Black = 20.

5. Two students from a student body of 30 boys and 50 girls will be selected to serve on the school disciplinary committee. What is the probability that first a boy will be chosen, and then a girl?
   a) 1/1500.
   b) 1500/6400.
   c) 1500/6320.
   d) 1.
   e) 30/50.

6. If number n, divided by number m, gives a result of .5, what is the relationship between n and m?
   a) n is twice as big as m.
   b) m is three times as big as n.
   c) n is a negative number.
   d) m is a negative number.
   e) n is ½ of m.

7. In a fruit basket, there are 10 apples, 5 oranges, 5 pears, and 6 figs. If I select two fruits, what is the probability that I will first pick a pear and then an apple?
   a) .07.
   b) .08.
   c) 1/13.
   d) 13.
   e) 5.

8. In a fruit basket, there are 3 apples, 5 oranges, 2 pears, and 2 figs. If I pick out two fruits, what is the probability that I will pick a fig first and then an apple?
   Round to the nearest 100th.
   a) .04.
   b) .05.
   c) .06.
   d) .03.
   e) .02.

9. If x workers can make p toys in c days, how many toys can y workers make in d days if they work at the same rate?
   a) cp/qx.
   b) cq/px.
   c) cqy/px.
   d) pdy/cx.
   e) qy/px.

10. If a car travels 35 miles on a gallon of gas, how far will it travel on 13 gallons of gas?
    a) 189 miles.
    b) 255 miles.
    c) 335 miles.
    d) 455 miles.
    e) 500 miles.

Test Your Knowledge: Ratios, Proportions, Rate of Change – Answers

1. **b)**
   The ratio of boys to girls is 150:100, or 3:2.

2. **b)**
   A full tank has 16 gallons → 3/4 of the tank = 12 gallons. The car can travel 30 miles on 4 gallons, so 12 gallons would take the car 12 * 30/4 = 90 miles.

3. **c)**
   Average Rate of Change = the change in value/change in time = (total profit – initial profit)/change in time. Initial profit = 0; change in time = 7 years.

   Increase = 5000 * 5 = 25000; decrease = 2000 * 2 = 4000; total profit = 25000 - 4000 = 21000.

   (21000 - 0)/7 years = $3000/year.

4. **c)**
   Total number of marbles = 250.

   #red marbles = 250 * 40/100 = 250 * .4 = 100.

   #blue marbles = 250 * .3 = 75.

   #green marbles = 250 * .1 = 25.

   #black marbles = 250 * .2 = 50.

5. **c)**
   The probability of selecting a boy from the entire group = 30:80.

   The probability of selecting a girl from the remaining group = 50:79.

   The probability of selecting a boy and a girl is (30:80) * (50:79) = 1500:6320.

6. **e)**
   If n/m = .5, then n = .5m, or n = ½ of m.

7. **c)**
   The total number of fruit = 26.

   The probability of picking a pear = 5:26.

   The probability of picking an apple = 10:25.

   The probability of picking a pear and an apple = 5:26 * 10:25 = 50:650 = 1:13.

8. b)

The total number of fruit $= 12$.

The probability of picking a fig $= 2:12$.

The probability of picking an apple $= 3:11$.

The probability of picking a fig and an apple $= 2:12 * 3:11 = 6:132 = .045$.

Round up to $.05$.

9. d)

The overall rate for x workers $=$ the number of toys/ the number of days, p/c. The number of toys one worker makes per day (rate) $= p/cx$. If q is the number of toys y workers make, and the rates are equal, then the number of toys made $=$ the rate x.

The number of days * the number of workers gives us $q = p/cx$ (dy), so:

$q = pdy/cx$.

10. d)

The distance travelled $= (35/1)(13) = 455$ miles.

Chapter 2: English and Language Arts

The first step in getting ready for this section of the test consists of reviewing the basic techniques used to determine the meanings of words you are not familiar with. The good news is that you have been using various degrees of these techniques since you first began to speak. Sharpening these skills will also help you with the ELA subtest.

Following each section you will find a practice drill. Use your score on these to determine if you need to study that particular subject matter further. At the end of the chapter you will find a review of the concepts and a chapter test. The questions found on the practice drills and chapter test are not given in the two formats found on the ELA subtest; rather they are designed to reinforce the skills needed to score well on the ELA subtest.

VOCABULARY and GRAMMAR

It's time to review those basic techniques used to determine the meanings of words with which you are not familiar. Don't worry though! The good news is that you have been using various degrees of these techniques since you first began to speak.

We have not included a vocabulary list in this book, because reading definitions from a page is the worst way to improve word knowledge. Interaction, and seeing the words used in context, is the best way to learn. We recommend using flashcards to improve your vocabulary knowledge – there are many resources available online. The best we've found is www.vocabulary.com/il; but you should find what suits you specifically!

Below are techniques for improving and utilizing the vocabulary you already have.

Context Clues

The most fundamental vocabulary skill is using the context of a word to determine its meaning. Your ability to observe sentences closely is extremely useful when it comes to understanding new vocabulary words.

Types of Context

There are two different types of context that can help you understand the meaning of unfamiliar words: **sentence context** and **situational context**. Regardless of which context is present, these types of questions are not really testing your knowledge of vocabulary; rather, they test your ability to comprehend the meaning of a word through its usage.

Situational context is context that comes from understanding the situation in which a word or phrase occurs.

Sentence context occurs within the sentence that contains the vocabulary word. To figure out words using sentence context clues, you should first determine the most important words in the sentence.

Example: I had a hard time reading her <u>illegible</u> handwriting.
a) Neat.
b) Unsafe.
c) Sloppy.
d) Educated.

Already, you know that this sentence is discussing something that is hard to read. Look at the word that **illegible** is describing: **handwriting**. Based on context clues, you can tell that illegible means that her handwriting is hard to read.

Next, look at the answer choices. Choice **a) Neat** is obviously a wrong answer because neat handwriting would not be difficult to read. Choice **b) Unsafe** and **d) Educated** don't make sense. Therefore, choice **c) Sloppy** is the best answer choice.

Types of Clues

There are four types of clues that can help you understand context, and therefore the meaning of a word. They are **restatement**, **positive/negative**, **contrast**, and **specific detail**.

Restatement clues occur when the definition of the word is clearly stated in the sentence.

Example: The dog was <u>dauntless</u> in the face of danger, braving the fire to save the girl.
a) Difficult.
b) Fearless.
c) Imaginative.

Demonstrating **bravery** in the face of danger would be **fearless,** choice **b)**. In this case, the context clues tell you exactly what the word means.

Positive/negative clues can tell you whether a word has a positive or negative meaning.

Example: The magazine gave a great review of the fashion show, stating the clothing was **sublime**.
    a) Horrible.
    b) Exotic.
    c) Bland
    d) Gorgeous.

The sentence tells us that the author liked the clothing enough to write a **great** review, so you know that the best answer choice is going to be a positive word. Therefore, you can immediately rule out choices **a)** and **c)** because they are negative words. **Exotic** is a neutral word; alone, it doesn't inspire a **great** review. The most positive word is gorgeous, which makes choice **d) Gorgeous** the best answer.

The following sentence uses both restatement and positive/negative clues:

"Janet suddenly found herself <u>destitute</u>, so poor she could barely afford to eat."

The second part of the sentence clearly indicates that destitute is a negative word; it also restates the meaning: very poor.

Contrast clues include the opposite meaning of a word. Words like **but, on the other hand,** and **however** are tip-offs that a sentence contains a contrast clue.

Example: Beth did not spend any time preparing for the test, but Tyron kept a <u>rigorous</u> study schedule.
    a) Strict.
    b) Loose.
    c) Boring.
    d) Strange.

In this case, the word **but** tells us that Tyron studied in a different way than Beth. If Beth did not study very hard, then Tyron did study hard for the test. The best answer here, therefore, is choice **a) Strict**.

Specific detail clues give a precise detail that can help you understand the meaning of the word.

Example: The box was heavier than he expected and it began to become <u>cumbersome</u>.
    a) Impossible.
    b) Burdensome.
    c) Obligated.
    d) Easier.

Start by looking at the specific details of the sentence. Choice **d)** can be eliminated right away because it is doubtful it would become **easier** to carry something that is **heavier**. There are also no clues in the sentence to indicate he was **obligated** to carry the box, so choice **c)** can also be disregarded. The sentence specifics, however, do tell you that the package was cumbersome because it was heavy to carry; something heavy to carry is a burden, which is **burdensome**, choice **b)**.

It is important to remember that more than one of these clues can be present in the same sentence. The more there are, the easier it will be to determine the meaning of the word, so look for them.

Denotation and Connotation

As you know, many English words have more than one meaning. For example, the word **quack** has two distinct definitions: the sound a duck makes; and a person who publicly pretends to have a skill, knowledge, education, or qualification which they do not possess.

The **denotations** of a word are the dictionary definitions.

The **connotations** of a word are the implied meaning(s) or emotion which the word makes you think.

> **Example**: "Sure," Pam said excitedly, "I'd just love to join your club; it sounds so exciting!"

> Now, read this sentence:

> "Sure," Pam said sarcastically, "I'd just love to join your club; it sounds so exciting!"

Even though the two sentences only differ by one word, they have completely different meanings. The difference, of course, lies in the words "excitedly" and "sarcastically."

Nouns, Pronouns, Verbs, Adjectives, and Adverbs

Nouns
Nouns are people, places, or things. They are typically the subject of a sentence. For example, "The hospital was very clean." The noun is "hospital;" it is the "place."

Pronouns
Pronouns essentially "replace" nouns. This allows a sentence to not sound repetitive. Take the sentence: "Sam stayed home from school because Sam was not feeling well." The word "Sam" appears twice in the same sentence. Instead, you can use a pronoun and say, "Sam stayed at home because *he* did not feel well." Sounds much better, right?

Most Common Pronouns:

- I, me, mine, my.

- You, your, yours.

- He, him, his.

- She, her, hers.

- It, its.

- We, us, our, ours.

- They, them, their, theirs.

Verbs
Remember the old commercial, "Verb: It's what you do"? That sums up verbs in a nutshell! Verbs are the "action" of a sentence; verbs "do" things.

They can, however, be quite tricky. Depending on the subject of a sentence, the tense of the word (past, present, future, etc.), and whether or not they are regular or irregular, verbs have many variations.

Example: "He runs to second base." The verb is "runs." This is a "regular verb."

Example: "I am 7 years old." The verb in this case is "am." This is an "irregular verb."

As mentioned, verbs must use the correct tense – and that tense must remain the same throughout the sentence. "I was baking cookies and eat some dough." That sounded strange, didn't it? That's because the two verbs "baking" and "eat" are presented in different tenses. "Was baking" occurred in the past; "eat," on the other hand, occurs in the present. Instead, it should be "**ate** some dough."

Adjectives
Adjectives are words that describe a noun and give more information. Take the sentence: "The boy hit the ball." If you want to know more about the noun "boy," then you could use an adjective to describe it.

73

"The **little** boy hit the ball." An adjective simply provides more information about a noun or subject in a sentence.

Adverb

For some reason, many people have a difficult time with adverbs – but don't worry! They are really quite simple. Adverbs are similar to adjectives in that they provide more information; however, they describe verbs, adjectives, and even other adverbs. They do **not** describe nouns – that's an adjective's job.

Take the sentence: "The doctor said she hired a new employee."

It would give more information to say: "The doctor said she **recently** hired a new employee." Now we know more about *how* the action was executed. Adverbs typically describe when or how something has happened, how it looks, how it feels, etc.

Good vs. Well

A very common mistake that people make concerning adverbs is the misuse of the word "good."

"Good" is an adjective – things taste good, look good, and smell good. "Good" can even be a noun – "Superman does good" – when the word is speaking about "good" vs. "evil." HOWEVER, "good" is never an adverb.

People commonly say things like, "I did really good on that test," or, "I'm good." Ugh! This is NOT the correct way to speak! In those sentences, the word "good" is being used to describe an action: how a person **did**, or how a person **is**. Therefore, the adverb "well" should be used. "I did really **well** on that test." "I'm **well**."

The correct use of "well" and "good" can make or break a person's impression of your grammar – make sure to always speak correctly!

The Parts of Words

Although you are not expected to know every word in the English language for your test, you will need to have the ability to use deductive reasoning to find the choice that is the best match for the word in question, which is why we are going to explain how to break a word into its parts of meaning

prefix – root – suffix

One trick in dividing a word into its parts is to first divide the word into its **syllables**. To show how syllables can help you find roots and affixes, we'll use the word **descendant,** which means one who comes from an ancestor. Start by dividing the word into its individual syllables; this word has three: **de-scend-ant**. The next step is to look at the beginning and end of the word, and then determine if these syllables are prefixes, suffixes, or possible roots. You can then use the meanings of each part to guide you in defining the word. When you divide words into their specific parts, they do not always add up to an exact definition, but you will see a relationship between their parts.

Note: This trick won't always work in every situation, because not all prefixes, roots, and suffixes have only one syllable. For example, take the word **monosyllabic** (which ironically means "one syllable"). There are five syllables in that word, but only three parts. The prefix is "mono," meaning "one." The root "syllab" refers to "syllable," while the suffix "ic" means "pertaining to." Therefore, we have one very long word which means "pertaining to one syllable."

The more familiar you become with these fundamental word parts, the easier it will be to define unfamiliar words. Although the words found on the Word Knowledge subtest are considered vocabulary words learned by the tenth grade level of high school, some are still less likely to be found in an individual's everyday vocabulary. The root and affixes list in this chapter uses more common words as examples to help you learn them more easily. Don't forget that you use word roots and affixes every day, without even realizing it. Don't feel intimidated by the long list of roots and affixes (prefixes and suffixes) at the end of this chapter, because you already know and use them every time you communicate with some else, verbally and in writing. If you take the time to read through the list just once a day for two weeks, you will be able to retain most of them and understand a high number of initially unfamiliar words.

Roots, Prefixes, and Suffixes

Roots
Roots are the building blocks of all words. Every word is either a root itself or has a root. Just as a plant cannot grow without roots, neither can vocabulary, because a word must have a root to give it meaning.

Example: The test instructions were **unclear.**

The root is what is left when you strip away all the prefixes and suffixes from a word. In this case, take away the prefix "un-," and you have the root **clear**.

Roots are not always recognizable words, because they generally come from Latin or Greek words, such as **nat**, a Latin root meaning **born**. The word native, which means a person born of a referenced placed, comes from this root, so does the word prenatal, meaning before birth. Yet, if you used the prefix **nat** instead of born, just on its own, no one would know what you were talking about.
Words can also have more than one root. For example, the word **omnipotent** means all powerful. Omnipotent is a combination of the roots **omni-**, meaning all or every, and **-potent**, meaning power or strength. In this case, **omni** cannot be used on its own as a single word, but **potent** can.

Again, it is important to keep in mind that roots do not always match the exact definitions of words and they can have several different spellings, but breaking a word into its parts is still one of the best ways to determine its meaning.

Prefixes

Prefixes are syllables added to the beginning of a word and suffixes are syllables added to the end of the word. Both carry assigned meanings. The common name for prefixes and suffixes is **affixes**. Affixes do not have to be attached directly to a root and a word can often have more than one prefix and/or suffix. Prefixes and suffixes can be attached to a word to completely change the word's meaning or to enhance the word's original meaning. Although they don't mean much to us on their own, when attached to other words affixes can make a world of difference.

Let's use the word **prefix** itself as an example:

Fix means to place something securely.

Pre means before.

Prefix means to place something before or in front.

Suffixes

Suffixes come after the root of a word.

Example: Feminism

Femin is a root. It means female, woman.

-ism means act, practice or process.

Feminism is the defining and establishing of equal political, economic, and social rights for women.

Unlike prefixes, **suffixes** can be used to change a word's part of speech.

Example: "Randy raced to the finish line." VS "Shana's costume was very racy."

In the first sentence, raced is a verb. In the second sentence, racy is an adjective. By changing the suffix from **-ed** to **-y**, the word race changes from a verb into an adjective, which has an entirely different meaning.

Although you cannot determine the meaning of a word by a prefix or suffix alone, you *can* use your knowledge of what root words mean to eliminate answer choices; indicating if the word is positive or negative can give you a partial meaning of the word.

Study Tips for Improving Vocabulary and Grammar

1. You're probably pretty computer savvy and know the Internet very well. Visit the Online Writing Lab website, which is sponsored by Purdue University, at http://owl.english.purdue.edu. This site provides you with an excellent overview of syntax, writing style, and strategy. It also has helpful and lengthy review sections that include multiple-choice "Test Your Knowledge" quizzes, which provide immediate answers to the questions.

2. It's beneficial to read the entire passage first to determine its intended meaning BEFORE you attempt to answer any questions. Doing so provides you with key insight into a passage's syntax (especially verb tense, subject-verb agreement, modifier placement, writing style, and punctuation).

3. When you answer a question, use the "Process-of-Elimination Method" to determine the best answer. Try each of the four answers and determine which one BEST fits with the meaning of the paragraph. Find the BEST answer. Chances are that the BEST answer is the CORRECT answer.

Test Your Knowledge: Vocabulary and Grammar

1. "The medication must be properly administered to the patient."
   Which of the words in the above sentence is an adverb?
   a) Medication.
   b) Properly.
   c) Administered.
   d) Patient.

2. "The old man had trouble walking if he did not have his walker and had a long way to go."
   What is the subject of the sentence?
   a) Walker.
   b) His.
   c) Trouble.
   d) Man.

3. "The boy decided ___ would ride his bike now that the sun was shining."
   Which of the following pronouns completes the sentence?
   a) His.
   b) Him.
   c) He.
   d) They.

4. "The impatient student hurried through the test and failed as a result."
   Which word is an adjective?
   a) Hurried.
   b) Result.
   c) Impatient.
   d) Student.

5. Correct the verb: "The nurse decided it were a good time to follow up with a patient about their medication."
   a) Was.
   b) Is.
   c) Has.
   d) No error.

Use context clues to determine the meaning of each underlined word.

6. His story didn't seem very realistic; even though it was a documentary.
   a) Believable.
   b) Humorous.
   c) Poetic.
   d) Exciting.

7. Listening to music too loudly, especially through headphones, can <u>impair</u> your hearing.
   a) Damage.
   b) Heighten.
   c) Use.
   d) Ensure.

8. Kelly's game happened to <u>coincide</u> with the Sue's recital.
   a) Happen before.
   b) Occur at the same time.
   c) Occur afterward.
   d) Not happen.

9. The weather has been very extreme lately; thankfully, today it's much more <u>temperate</u>.
   a) Troubling.
   b) Beautiful.
   c) Cold.
   d) Moderate.

10. He knew he couldn't win the race after falling off his bike, so he had to <u>concede</u>.
   a) Continue.
   b) Give up.
   c) Challenge.
   d) Be thankful.

11. The editor, preferring a more <u>terse</u> writing style, cut 30% of the words from the article.
   a) Elegant.
   b) Factual.
   c) Descriptive.
   d) Concise.

12. Victor Frankenstein spent the last years of his life chasing his <u>elusive</u> monster, which was always one step ahead.
   a) Unable to be compared.
   b) Unable to be captured.
   c) Unable to be forgotten.
   d) Unable to be avoided.

13. Certain <u>passages</u> were taken from the book for the purpose of illustration.
   a) Excerpts.
   b) Contents.
   c) Paragraphs.
   d) Tables.

14. The investigator searched among the <u>ruins</u> for the cause of the fire.
   a) Terminal.
   b) Foundation.
   c) Rubble.
   d) Establishment.

15. To make her novels more engaging, Cynthia was known to <u>embellish</u> her writing with fictitious details.
   a) Add to.
   b) Detract.
   c) Isolate.
   d) Disavow.

16. Robert's well-timed joke served to <u>diffuse</u> the tension in the room and the party continued happily.
   a) Refuse.
   b) Intensify.
   c) Create.
   d) Soften.

17. I had a difficult time understanding the book because the author kept <u>digressing</u> to unrelated topics.
   a) Deviating, straying.
   b) Regressing, reverting.
   c) Changing the tone.
   d) Expressing concisely.

18. The senator <u>evaded</u> almost every question.
   a) Avoided.
   b) Answered indirectly.
   c) Refused to answer directly.
   d) Deceived.

19. Sammie hasn't come out of her room all afternoon, but I would <u>surmise</u> that it is because she is upset about not being able to go to the mall.
   a) Confirm.
   b) Surprise.
   c) Believe.
   d) Guess.

20. The details can be worked out later; what's important is that the company follows the <u>crux</u> of the argument, which is that everyone be paid equally.
   a) Overall tone.
   b) Specific fact.
   c) Main point.
   d) Logic, reasoning.

Use context clues to choose the best word to complete the sentence.

21. Mr. Collins _____ tomatoes so vehemently that he felt ill just smelling them.
   a) Resented
   b) Disliked
   c) Detested
   d) Hated

22. We were rolling on the ground with laughter during the _____ new movie.
- a) Comical
- b) Humorous
- c) Amusing
- d) Hilarious

23. Tina's parents made us feel right at home during our visit to their house with their generous _____.
- a) Unselfishness
- b) Politeness
- c) Hospitality
- d) Charity

24. Although his mother was not happy that he broke the window, she was pleased that he was _____ about it.
- a) Honest
- b) Trustworthy
- c) Authentic
- d) Decent

25. The soldiers _____ to their feet immediately when then officer walked into the room.
- a) Stood
- b) Leapt
- c) Rose
- d) Skipped

Try to find the root in each of the underlined words.

26. The bridge was out, so the river was <u>impassable</u>.
- a) Im-
- b) -pass-
- c) -a-
- d) –able

27. I am usually on time, but my husband is <u>chronically</u> late.
- a) Chron-
- b) -chronical-
- c) -ally-
- d) -ic

28. The only way to succeed is by <u>striving</u> to do your best.
- a) Str-
- a) Striv-
- b) Strive-
- c) -ing

29. We drifted along lazily on the <u>tranquil</u> river.
- a) Tra-
- b) -qui-
- c) Tranq-
- d) -uil

30. A <u>pediatrician</u> is a doctor who takes care of children.
- a) Ped-
- b) -ia-
- c) -tri-
- d) -cian

Choose the word that shares the same root as the given word.

31. Audible:
- a) Auditorium.
- b) Because.
- c) Dribble.
- d) Bagel.

32. Nominate:
- a) Eaten.
- b) Minute.
- c) Hated.
- d) Synonym.

33. Disappoint:
- a) Disappear.
- b) Appointment.
- c) Interest.
- d) Potato.

34. Dilute:
- a) Flute.
- b) Dictate.
- c) Pollute.
- d) Hesitate.

35. Sympathy:
- a) System.
- b) Empathy.
- c) Pattern.
- d) Rhythm.

36. Science:
   a) Conscious.
   b) Once.
   c) Alien.
   d) Parasite.

37. Incline:
   a) Recline.
   b) Independent.
   c) Cluster.
   d) Twine.

For each question below, use the Latin root to determine the meaning of the underlined word.

38. An amiable person is:
   a) Talkative, loud.
   b) Truthful, honest.
   c) Highly educated.
   d) Friendly, good-natured.

39. A lucid argument:
   a) Is very clear and intelligible.
   b) Is loosely held together, tenuous.
   c) Frequently digresses.
   d) Errs repeatedly in its logic.

40. A complacent person:
   a) Frequently makes mistakes, but does not accept responsibility.
   b) Likes to pick fights.
   c) Is contented to a fault, self-satisfied.
   d) Is known to tell lies, embellish the truth.

41. To exacerbate a problem means:
   a) To solve it.
   b) To analyze it.
   c) To lessen it.
   d) To worsen it.

42. To measure the veracity of something is to measure its:
   a) Value or worth.
   b) Truthfulness.
   c) Weight.
   d) Life force.

43. Something that is eloquent is:
   a) Dull, trite, hackneyed.
   b) Expressed in a powerful and effective manner.
   c) Very old, antiquated.
   d) Equally divided or apportioned.

44. To <u>indict</u> someone is to:
- a) Pick a fight with that person.
- b) Stop or block that person from doing something.
- c) Charge that person with a crime.
- d) Love that person dearly.

45. A <u>quiescent</u> place is:
- a) Very isolated.
- b) Tumultuous, chaotic.
- c) Sacred.
- d) Still, at rest.

What are the affixes in each word?

46. Disease:
- a) Dis-.
- b) -ise-.
- c) -eas-.
- d) –ase.

47. Uncomfortable:
- a) Un-.
- b) Un-, -com-.
- c) -fort-.
- d) Un-, -able.

48. Disrespected:
- a) Re-, -spect, -ed.
- b) Dis-, -ed.
- c) Dis-, re-, -ed.
- d) Respect-, -ed.

49. Impressive:
- a) Im-, -ive.
- b) –ive.
- c) Press-, -ive.
- d) Impre-, -ive.

50. Predated:
- a) Pre-.
- b) Pre-, -d.
- c) Pre-, -ed.
- d) –d.

Using your knowledge of prefixes and root words, try to determine the meaning of the words in the following questions.

51. To take <u>precaution</u> is to:
- a) Prepare before doing something.
- b) Remember something that happened earlier.
- c) Become aware of something for the first time.
- d) Try to do something again.

52. To <u>reorder</u> a list is to:
- a) Use the same order again.
- b) Put the list in a new order.
- c) Get rid of the list.
- d) Find the list.

53. An <u>antidote</u> to a disease is:
- a) Something that is part of the disease.
- b) Something that works against the disease.
- c) Something that makes the disease worse.
- d) Something that has nothing to do with the disease.

54. Someone who is <u>multiethnic</u>:
- a) Likes only certain kinds of people.
- b) Lives in the land of his or her birth.
- c) Is from a different country.
- d) Has many different ethnicities.

55. Someone who is <u>misinformed</u> has been:
- a) Taught something new.
- b) Told the truth.
- c) Forgotten.
- d) Given incorrect information.

Choose the best answer to each question. (Remember you are looking for the closest meaning.)

56. <u>Exorbitant</u> means:
- a) Belonging to a group.
- b) To orbit.
- c) Beneath conscious awareness.
- d) Far beyond what is normal or reasonable.

57. <u>Denunciation</u> means:
- a) To denounce or openly condemn.
- b) Critical, of or like a condemnation.
- c) One who denounces or openly condemns another.
- d) The act of denouncing or openly condemning.

58. Metamorphosis means:
   a) To transform.
   b) One who has changed.
   c) A transformation.
   d) Tending to change frequently.

59. To reconcile means:
   a) To reestablish a close relationship between.
   b) To move away from.
   c) To undermine.
   d) To surpass or outdo.

60. Didactic means:
   a) A teacher or instructor.
   b) Intended to instruct, moralizing.
   c) To preach or moralize.
   d) The process of instructing.

61. Unilateral means:
   a) To multiply.
   b) Understated.
   c) Literal.
   d) One-sided.

62. Subordinate means:
   a) Under someone else's authority or control.
   b) Organized according to rank; hierarchical.
   c) Something ordinary or average, without distinction.
   d) Repeated frequently to aid memorization.

63. Incisive means:
   a) Insight.
   b) Worthy of consideration.
   c) Penetrating.
   d) To act forcefully.

64. Intermittent means:
   a) Badly handled.
   b) Occurring at intervals
   c) Greatly varied.
   d) A number between one and ten.

65. Miscreant means:
   a) Someone who is unconventional.
   b) Someone who lacks creativity.
   c) A very naive person.
   d) An evil person or villain.

Test Your Knowledge: Vocabulary and Grammar – Answers

1. b)
"Properly" is the adverb which describes the verb "administered."

2. d)
Although there are other nouns in the sentence, the "man" is the subject.

3. c)
"He" is the correct answer; the other pronouns are possessive or otherwise in the wrong tense.

4. c)
"Impatient" describes the noun "student."

5. a)
"Was" is the correct answer; the other choices are in the wrong tense.

6. a) Believable.
Realistic means accurate, truthful, and believable.

7. a) Damage.
This is the only logical choice.

8. b) Occur at the same time.
According to information in the sentence, the game was scheduled at the same time as the recital.

9. d) Moderate.
The context says that the weather has been "extreme." It does not say if the weather has been extremely hot or cold; therefore, choices **b) Beautiful** and **c) Cold** can be ruled out. The sentence also indicates a change from negative to positive making moderate the best choice.

10. b) Give up.
The speaker of the sentence knows they cannot win, so choice **b)** is the best choice.

11. d) Concise.
Terse means concise, using no unnecessary words. The main clue is that the editor cut words from the article, reducing its wordiness.

12. b) Unable to be captured.
Elusive means evasive, difficult to capture.

13. a) Excerpt.
An excerpt is a passage or quote from a book, article, or other publication

14. c) Rubble is synonymous with ruin.

15. a) Add to.

To embellish is to add details to a story to make it more appealing.

16. d) Soften.

The clues *tension* and *continue happily* tell you that **d)** is the best choice

17. a) To deviate, stray.

To digress means to deviate; to stray from the main subject in writing or speaking.

18. a) To avoid.

To evade means to avoid by cleverness. The senator avoids answering the question by changing the subject.

19. d) Guess.

The speaker is guessing why Samantha is upset based on circumstances; she has not actually given a reason.

20. c) Main point.

Crux means the central or main point, especially of a problem. The main context clue is that the speaker isn't concerned with the details but is focused on getting agreement on the main point.

21. c) Detested.

The knowledge that Mr. Collins feels ill just smelling tomatoes suggests that his hatred for tomatoes is intense; therefore, the best choice will be the most negative. To **dislike** tomatoes – choice **b)** – is the most neutral word, so this choice can be ruled out. **Resented** is a word that generally applies to people or their actions, ruling out choice **a)**. Given the choice between **c)** and **d),** the most negative is **c) Detested**.

22. d) Hilarious.

The movie must be extremely funny for the audience to have this sort of reaction, and, while all of the answer choices are synonyms for funny, the only one that means extremely funny is choice **d) Hilarious**.

23. c) Hospitality.

Although all four choices describe different types of kindness, **unselfishness** – choice **a)** – can be ruled out because it has the same basic meaning as the adjective, generous. Choice **d) Charity** is a kindness usually associated with those less fortunate; since nothing in the context indicates this type of relationship, this choice can also be eliminated.

Left with choices **b) Politeness** and **c) Hospitality**, hospitality best describes the kindness of welcoming someone into your home.

24. a) Honest.

Again we have a case in which all of the word choices are synonyms for the word honest. In this case, the most neutral word is the best choice. Choice **b) Trustworthy**, **c) Authentic**, and **d) Decent** do not make as much sense as the most basic synonym, **honest**.

25. b) Leapt. The word immediately is the main clue. **a) Stood** and **c) Rose** are neutral words that do not convey a sense of urgency. Choice **b) Leapt** is the only word that implies the immediacy demanded by the sentence context.

26. b) –pass- .

27. a) Chron-.

28. c) Strive-.

29. b) –qui-.
Quies is a Latin root meaning rest or quiet.

30. a) Ped-.
Ped is a Latin root meaning child or education. You might recognize that the suffix **-cian** refers to what someone does, such as physician or beautician. The suffix **-iatr** relates to doctors, as you can see in the words psychiatry and podiatry. Both suffixes support the root of the word.

31. a) Auditorium.
From the Latin root **aud**, meaning hearing or listening.

32. d) Synonym.
The words nominate and synonym share the root, **nom**, meaning name. Remember, roots are not necessarily going to be in the same position in other words.

33. b) Appointment.
Greek root **poie**, meaning to make.

34. c) Pollute.
Both dilute and pollute come from the root **lut**, meaning to wash.

35. b) Empathy.
The words sympathy and empathy come from the Greek root **path,** meaning feeling, suffering, or disease.

36. a) Conscious.
Science and conscious share the Latin root **sci,** which means to know.

37. a) Recline.
The words incline and recline both share the Greek root *clin,* meaning to lean toward or bend.

38. d)
The root **am** means love. Amiable means friendly and agreeable or good natured, likeable, or pleasing.

39. a)
The root **luc/lum/lus** means light. Lucid means very clear, easy to understand, intelligible.

40. c)

The root **plac** means to please. Complacent means contented to a fault; self-satisfied (pleased with oneself).

41. d) The root **ac** means sharp, bitter. To exacerbate means to make worse or to increase the severity, violence, or bitterness of.

42. b)

The root **ver** means truth. Veracity means truth or truthfulness.

43. b)

The root **loc/log/loqu** means word or speech. Eloquent means expressed in a powerful, fluent, and persuasive manner.

44. c)

The root **dic/dict/dit** means to say, tell, or use words. To indict means to formally accuse of or charge with a crime.

45. d)

The root **qui** means quiet. Quiescent means inactive, quiet, or at rest.

46. a) Dis-.

The prefix **dis-** means away from, deprive of, reversal, or not. If someone has a **disease** they are not well.

47. d) Un-, -able.

The prefix **un-** means not. The suffix **-able** means ability or worthy of. **Uncomfortable** means not able to be in a state of comfort.

48. c) Dis-, re-, -ed.

The prefix **dis-** means away from, reversal, or not. The prefix **re-** means back or again. The suffix **-ed** indicates that the word is in the past tense. **Disrespected** means showed a lack of respect towards.

49. a) Im-, -ive.

The prefix **im-** means in, into, or within. The suffix **-ive** means having the nature of. **Impressive** means having the ability inspire an internal feeling of awe.

50. c) Pre-, -ed.

The prefix **pre-** means before. The suffix **-ed** indicates that the word is in the past tense. **Predated** means came before the date.

51. a) Prepare before doing something.

Pre- means before; to take **caution** is to be careful or take heed.

52. b) Put the list in a new order.

Re- means again. In this case, order means organize. Reorder then means to organize the list again or to put the list into a different order.

53. b) Something that works against the disease.
The prefix **anti-** means against. An **antidote** is something that works against a disease or a poison.

54. d) Has many different ethnicities.
The prefix **multi-** means many. Someone who is **multiethnic** has relatives from many different ethnic groups.

55. d) Given incorrect information.
Mis- means opposite, and to be **informed** is to have the correct information.

56. d) Far beyond what is normal or reasonable.
The prefix **ex-** means out, out of, away from.

57. a) The act of denouncing or openly condemning.
The prefix **de-** means against, the root **nounc** means to state or declare, and the noun suffix **-tion** means the act or state of.

58. c) A transformation.
The prefix **meta-** means change, while the root **morph** means shape or form, and the **noun** suffix **-sis** means the process of. **Metamorphosis** means a marked change of form or a transformation.

59. a) Means to reestablish a relationship.
The prefix **re-** means back or again and, the root **con** means with. Together they mean back together again or reestablishing a relationship.

60. b) Intended to instruct or moralize.
The adjective suffix **-ic** means pertaining or relating to, having the quality of. Only choices **b)** and **d)** define a quality, and choice **d)** would require an additional suffix.

61. d) One-sided.
The prefix **uni-** means one.

62. a) Under someone else's authority or control.
The prefix **sub-** means under, beneath or below.

63. c) Penetrating.
The adjective suffix **-ive** means having the nature of.

64. b) Occurring at intervals.
The prefix **inter-** means between or among.

65. d) An evil person or villain.
The prefix **mis-** means bad, evil, or wrong. The suffix **–ant** means an agent or something that performs the action.

Chapter 3: Reading

There are three types of questions that you can encounter in the Reading Comprehension section of the TEAS:

1. **About the Author**: The question will ask about the author's attitude, thoughts, opinions, etc. When encountering a question asking specifically about the author, pay attention to context clues in the article. The answer may not be explicitly stated, but instead conveyed in the overall message.

2. **Passage Facts**: You must distinguish between facts and opinions presented in the passage. Remember, a fact is something verifiable or proven, whereas an opinion is simply a belief that cannot be proven for sure. For example: "The sky is blue" is a fact that cannot be argued; "the sky is a prettier blue today than it was yesterday" is an opinion, since there is no scientific basis for what makes the sky "prettier" to a person.

3. **Additional Information**: These questions will have you look at what kind of information could be added to or was missing from the passage. They may also ask in what direction the passage was going. Questions may ask what statement could be added to strengthen the author's statement, or weaken it; they may also provide a fill-in-the-blank option to include a statement that is missing from, but fits with the rest of, the passage. When looking over answer choices, read them with the passage to see if they sound correct in context.

Strategies

Despite the different types of questions you will face, there are some strategies for Reading Comprehension which apply across the board:

- **Read the Answer Choices First**, then read the passage. This will save you time, as you will know what to look out for as you read.

- **Use the Process of Elimination**. Some answer choices are obviously incorrect, and are relatively easy to detect. After reading the passage, eliminate those blatantly-incorrect answer choices; this increases your chance of finding the correct answer much more quickly.

- **Avoid "Negatives."** Generally, test-makers will not make negatives statements about anyone or anything. Statements will be either neutral or positive; so if it seems like an answer choice is making a negative connotation, it is very likely that the answer is intentionally false.

Here are some examples of the kinds of questions you may encounter in the Reading Section. Each passage will have at least one of the above listed question types – try to answer them for yourself before reading the solution. If you run into trouble, don't worry. We'll provide more practice drills later in the book, as well.

Sample One:

Exercise is a critical aspect for healthy development in children. Today, there is an epidemic of unhealthy children in the United States who will face health problems in adulthood due to poor diet and lack of exercise as children. This is a problem for all Americans, especially with the rising cost of health care.

It is vital that school systems and parents encourage their children to engage in a minimum of 30 minutes of cardiovascular exercise each day, meaning their heart rate is mildly increased for sustained period. This is proven to decrease the likelihood of development diabetes, becoming obese, and a multitude of other health problems. Also, children need a proper diet rich in fruits and vegetables so that they can grow and development physically, as well as learn healthy eating habits early on.

1. Which of the following describes the author's use of the word "vital"?
   a) Debatable.
   b) Very important.
   c) Somewhat important.
   d) Not important.
   e) Indicator.

Answer: This is an example of an "About the Author" question. You can tell, from both the tone and the intention of the article, that the author feels very strongly about the health of children and that action should be taken. Therefore, answer **b)** is the correct choice.

2. Which of the following is a fact in the passage, not an opinion?
   a) Fruits and vegetables are the best-tasting foods.
   b) Children today are lazier than they were in previous generations.
   c) The risk of diabetes in children is reduced by physical activity.
   d) Health care costs too much.
   e) Soccer is a better physical activity than tennis.

Answer: A fact is typically presented as a direct statement, not a comparison, which makes answer choice **c)** the correct answer. Notice that many of the incorrect answers contain words that can hint at it being an opinion such as "best," "better," "too much," or other comparisons. Also keep an eye out for answer choices that may be facts, but which are not stated in the passage.

3. What other information might the author have provided to strengthen the argument?
   a) Example of fruits and vegetables children should eat.
   b) How much health insurance costs today vs. 10 years ago.
   c) How many people live in the United States today.
   d) The rules of baseball and soccer.
   e) How many calories the average person burns by running 1 mile.

Answer: All of the choices would provide additional information, but only one pertains specifically to the improvement of health in children: choice **a)**.

Sample Two:

My "office" measures a whopping 5 feet by 7 feet. A large desk is squeezed into one corner, leaving just enough room for a rickety chair between the desk and the wall. Yellow paint is peeling off the walls in dirty chunks. The ceiling is barely six feet tall; it's like a hat that I wear all day long. The window, a single 2 x 2 pane, looks out onto a solid brick wall just two feet away.

1. What is the main idea implied by this paragraph?
   a) This office is small but comfortable.
   b) This office is in need of repair.
   c) This office is old and claustrophobic.
   d) This office is large and luxurious.
   e) None of the above.

Answer: Notice that all of the sentences in the passage relate to the office feeling small and cramped. The correct answer is choice **c)**. While choice **b)** is tempting, since one would think the office could use some repair, it is not the main point of the passage.

2. Which of the following describes the structure of the passage?
   a) The passage asks a question, then explains the answer using supporting arguments.
   b) The passage presents a statement, then follows with more detailed information.
   c) The passage makes an argument, then provides three examples to support it.
   d) The passage introduces a hypothesis, then explores more questions about the hypothesis.
   e) The passage starts with an argument, which is countered with a different argument leaving the reader to make their own conclusion.

Answer: No questions, arguments, or hypothesis were provided anywhere in the passage. Simply a statement of the size of the office and then additional details were given afterward. The correct answer is choice **b)**.

3. What is the author's meaning of the use of the word "hat" in the passage?
   a) An expression of a style of clothing the author prefers.
   b) To illustrate how very close the ceiling is to the author's head.
   c) The author does not like to wear hats, especially all day.
   d) The author enjoys wearing hats.
   e) None of the above.

Answer: The author uses the word "hat" to describe how low the ceiling sits in the office: that it feels as though it envelopes their head, much like a hat. While it can be inferred that the author does not like their office, there is no indication of whether the author likes or dislikes hats. The correct answer is choice **b)**.

Sample Three

1. Using the below Index, on which page would you find information on Organic Chemistry?

> **Science**
>> Geology: 110-124
>> Astronomy: 126-137
>> Physics: 140-159
>> Chemistry: 161-170
>> Biology: 171-179
>
> **Math**
>> Geometry: 201-209
>> Calculus: 210-222
>> Graphing: 225-251

    a) 210-222
    b) 225-251
    c) 126-137
    d) 161-170
    e) None of the above

Answer: The correct answer is choice **d)**. Pretty simple, huh? These types of questions are the easiest that you will find on the TEAS. Simply look for key-words (in this case "Chemistry" is the only matching word), and then eliminate everything else that doesn't relate.

REVIEW: READING

This section will measure your ability to understand, analyze, and evaluate written passages. The passages will contain material from a variety of sources, and will cover a number of different topics.

The Main Idea

Finding and understanding the main idea of a text is an essential reading skill. When you look past the facts and information and get to the heart of what the writer is trying to say, that's the **main idea**.

Imagine that you're at a friend's home for the evening:

> "Here," he says, "Let's watch this movie."

> "Sure," you reply. "What's it about?"

You'd like to know a little about what you'll be watching, but your question may not get you a satisfactory answer, because you've only asked about the subject of the film. The subject—what the movie is about—is only half the story. Think, for example, about all the alien invasion films ever been made. While these films may share the same general subject, what they have to say about the aliens or about humanity's theoretical response to invasion may be very different. Each film has different ideas it wants to convey about a subject, just as writers write because they have something they want to say about a particular subject. When you look beyond the facts and information to what the writer really wants to say about his or her subject, you're looking for the main idea.

One of the most common questions on reading comprehension exams is, "What is the main idea of this passage?" How would you answer this question for the paragraph below?

> "Wilma Rudolph, the crippled child who became an Olympic running champion, is an inspiration for us all. Born prematurely in 1940, Wilma spent her childhood battling illness, including measles, scarlet fever, chicken pox, pneumonia, and polio, a crippling disease which at that time had no cure. At the age of four, she was told she would never walk again. But Wilma and her family refused to give up. After years of special treatment and physical therapy, 12-year-old Wilma was able to walk normally again. But walking wasn't enough for Wilma, who was determined to be an athlete. Before long, her talent earned her a spot in the 1956 Olympics, where she earned a bronze medal. In the 1960 Olympics, the height of her career, she won three gold medals."

What is the main idea of this paragraph? You might be tempted to answer, "Wilma Rudolph" or "Wilma Rudolph's life." Yes, Wilma Rudolph's life is the **subject** of the passage—who or what the passage is about—but the subject is not necessarily the main idea. The **main idea** is what the writer wants to say about this subject. What is the main thing the writer says about Wilma's life?

Which of the following statements is the main idea of the paragraph?

> a) Wilma Rudolph was very sick as a child.
> b) Wilma Rudolph was an Olympic champion.
> c) Wilma Rudolph is someone to admire.

Main idea: The overall fact, feeling, or thought a writer wants to convey about his or her subject.

The best answer is **c)**: Wilma Rudolph is someone to admire. This is the idea the paragraph adds up to; it's what holds all of the information in the paragraph together. This example also shows two important characteristics of a main idea:

1. It is **general** enough to encompass all of the ideas in the passage.

2. It is an **assertion.** An assertion is a statement made by the writer.

The main idea of a passage must be general enough to encompass all of the ideas in the passage. It should be broad enough for all of the other sentences in that passage to fit underneath it, like people under an umbrella. Notice that the first two options, "Wilma Rudolph was very sick as a child" and "Wilma Rudolph was an Olympic champion", are too specific to be the main idea. They aren't broad enough to cover all of the ideas in the passage, because the passage talks about both her illnesses and her Olympic achievements. Only the third answer is general enough to be the main idea of the paragraph.

A main idea is also some kind of **assertion** about the subject. An assertion is a claim that something is true. Assertions can be facts or opinions, but in either case, an assertion should be supported by specific ideas, facts, and details. In other words, the main idea makes a general assertion that tells readers that something is true.

The supporting sentences, on the other hand, show readers that this assertion is true by providing specific facts and details. For example, in the Wilma Rudolph paragraph, the writer makes a general assertion: "Wilma Rudolph, the crippled child who became an Olympic running champion, is an inspiration for us all." The other sentences offer specific facts and details that prove why Wilma Rudolph is an inspirational person.

Writers often state their main ideas in one or two sentences so that readers can have a very clear understanding about the main point of the passage. A sentence that expresses the main idea of a paragraph is called a **topic sentence.**

Notice, for example, how the first sentence in the Wilma Rudolph paragraph states the main idea:

> "Wilma Rudolph, the crippled child who became an Olympic running champion, is an inspiration for us all."

This sentence is therefore the topic sentence for the paragraph. Topic sentences are often found at the beginning of paragraphs. Sometimes, though, writers begin with specific supporting ideas and lead up to the main idea, and in this case the topic sentence is often found at the end of the paragraph. Sometimes the topic sentence is even found somewhere in the middle, and other times there isn't a clear topic sentence at all—but that doesn't mean there isn't a main idea; the author has just chosen not to express it in a clear topic sentence. In this last case, you'll have to look carefully at the paragraph for clues about the main idea.

Main Ideas vs. Supporting Ideas

If you're not sure whether something is a main idea or a supporting idea, ask yourself the following question: is the sentence making a **general statement,** or is it providing **specific information?** In the Wilma Rudolph paragraph above, for example, all of the sentences except the first make specific statements. They are not general enough to serve as an umbrella or net for the whole paragraph.

Writers often provide clues that can help you distinguish between main ideas and their supporting ideas. Here are some of the most common words and phrases used to introduce specific examples:

1. **For example...**

2. **Specifically...**

3. **In addition...**

4. **Furthermore...**

5. **For instance...**

6. **Others...**

7. **In particular...**

8. **Some...**

These signal words tell you that a supporting fact or idea will follow. If you're having trouble finding the main idea of a paragraph, try eliminating sentences that begin with these phrases, because they will most likely be too specific to be a main ideas.

Implied Main Idea

When the main idea is **implied**, there's no topic sentence, which means that finding the main idea requires some detective work. But don't worry! You already know the importance of structure, word choice, style, and tone. Plus, you know how to read carefully to find clues, and you know that these clues will help you figure out the main idea.

For Example:

"One of my summer reading books was *The Windows of Time*. Though it's more than 100 pages long, I read it in one afternoon. I couldn't wait to see what happened to Evelyn, the main character. But by the time I got to the end, I wondered if I should have spent my afternoon doing something else. The ending was so awful that I completely forgot that I'd enjoyed most of the book."

There's no topic sentence here, but you should still be able to find the main idea. Look carefully at what the writer says and how she says it. What is she suggesting?

a) *The Windows of Time* is a terrific novel.
b) *The Windows of Time* is disappointing.
c) *The Windows of Time* is full of suspense.
d) *The Windows of Time* is a lousy novel.

The correct answer is **b)** – the novel is disappointing. How can you tell that this is the main idea? First, we can eliminate choice **c)**, because it's too specific to be a main idea. It deals only with one specific aspect of the novel (its suspense).

Sentences **a)**, **b)**, and **d)**, on the other hand, all express a larger idea – a general assertion about the quality of the novel. But only one of these statements can actually serve as a "net" for the whole paragraph. Notice that while the first few sentences praise the novel, the last two criticize it. Clearly, this is a mixed review.

Therefore, the best answer is **b)**. Sentence **a)** is too positive and doesn't account for the "awful" ending. Sentence **d)**, on the other hand, is too negative and doesn't account for the reader's sense of suspense and interest in the main character. But sentence **b)** allows for both positive and negative aspects – when a good thing turns bad, we often feel disappointed.

Now let's look at another example. Here, the word choice will be more important, so read carefully.

"Fortunately, none of Toby's friends had ever seen the apartment where Toby lived with his mother and sister. Sandwiched between two burnt-out buildings, his two-story apartment building was by far the ugliest one on the block. It was a real eyesore: peeling orange paint (orange!), broken windows, crooked steps, crooked everything. He could just imagine what his friends would say if they ever saw this poor excuse for a building."

Which of the following expresses the main idea of this paragraph?

- a) Toby wishes he could move to a nicer building.
- b) Toby wishes his dad still lived with them.
- c) Toby is glad none of his friends know where he lives.
- d) Toby is sad because he doesn't have any friends.

From the description, we can safely assume that Toby doesn't like his apartment building and wishes he could move to a nicer building **a)**. But that idea isn't general enough to cover the whole paragraph, because it's about his building.

Because the first sentence states that Toby has friends, the answer cannot be **d)**. We know that Toby lives only with his mother and little sister, so we might assume that he wishes his dad still lived with them, **b)**, but there's nothing in the paragraph to support that assumption, and this idea doesn't include the two main topics of the paragraph—Toby's building and Toby's friends.

What the paragraph adds up to is that Toby is terribly embarrassed about his building, and he's glad that none of his friends have seen it **c)**. This is the main idea. The paragraph opens with the word "fortunately," so we know that he thinks it's a good thing none of his friends have been to his house. Plus, notice how the building is described: "by far the ugliest on the block," which says a lot since it's stuck "between two burnt-out buildings." The writer calls it an "eyesore," and repeats "orange" with an exclamation point to emphasize how ugly the color is. Everything is "crooked" in this "poor excuse for a building." Toby is clearly ashamed of where he lives and worries about what his friends would think if they saw it.

Cause and Effect

Understanding cause and effect is important for reading success. Every event has at least one cause (what made it happen) and at least one effect (the result of what happened). Some events have more than one cause, and some have more than one effect. An event is also often part of a chain of causes and effects. Causes and effects are usually signaled by important transitional words and phrases.

Words Indicating Cause:

1. **Because (of)**

2. **Created (by)**

3. **Caused (by)**

4. **Since**

Words Indicating Effect:

1. **As a result**

2. **Since**

3. **Consequently**

4. **So**

5. **Hence**

6. **Therefore**

Sometimes, a writer will offer his or her opinion about why an event happened when the facts of the cause(s) aren't clear. Or a writer may predict what he or she thinks will happen because of a certain event (its effects). If this is the case, you need to consider how reasonable those opinions are. Are the writer's ideas logical? Does the writer offer support for the conclusions he or she offers?

Reading Between the Lines

Paying attention to word choice is particularly important when the main idea of a passage isn't clear. A writer's word choice doesn't just affect meaning; it also creates it. For example, look at the following description from a teacher's evaluation of a student applying to a special foreign language summer camp. There's no topic sentence, but if you use your powers of observation, you should be able to tell how the writer feels about her subject.

> "As a student, Jane usually completes her work on time and checks it carefully. She speaks French well and is learning to speak with less of an American accent. She has often been a big help to other students who are just beginning to learn the language."

What message does this passage send about Jane? Is she the best French student the writer has ever had? Is she one of the worst, or is she just average? To answer these questions, you have to make an inference, and you must support your inference with specific observations. What makes you come to the conclusion that you come to?

The **diction** of the paragraph above reveals that this is a positive evaluation, but not a glowing recommendation.

Here are some of the specific observations you might have made to support this conclusion:

- The writer uses the word "usually" in the first sentence. This means that Jane is good about meeting deadlines for work, but not great; she doesn't always hand in her work on time.

- The first sentence also says that Jane checks her work carefully. While Jane may sometimes hand in work late, at least she always makes sure it's quality work. She's not sloppy.

- The second sentence tells us she's "learning to speak with less of an American accent." This suggests that she has a strong accent and needs to improve in this area. It also suggests, though, that she is already making progress.

- The third sentence tells us that she "often" helps "students who are just beginning to learn the language." From this we can conclude that Jane has indeed mastered the basics. Otherwise, how could she be a big help to students who are just starting to learn? By looking at the passage carefully, then, you can see how the writer feels about her subject.

Test Your Knowledge: Reading

Remember to read the questions first, make sure that you read ALL answer choices ALL THE WAY THROUGH, and use process of elimination to make your job of selecting the correct answer easier. If you can answer a majority of these questions correctly, you are likely ready for the Reading Section of the TEAS.

Read each of the following paragraphs carefully and answer the questions that follow.

My "office" measures a whopping 5 x 7 feet. A large desk is squeezed into one corner, leaving just enough room for a rickety chair between the desk and the wall. Yellow paint is peeling off the walls in dirty chunks. The ceiling is barely six feet tall; it's like a hat that I wear all day long. The window, a single 2 x 2 pane, looks out onto a solid brick wall just two feet away.

1. What is the main idea implied by this paragraph?
    a) This office is small but comfortable.
    b) This office is in need of repair.
    c) This office is old and claustrophobic.
    d) None of the above.

There are many things you can do to make tax time easier. The single most important strategy is to keep accurate records. Keep all of your pay stubs, receipts, bank statements, and other relevant financial information in a neat, organized folder so that when you're ready to prepare your form, all of your paperwork is in one place. The second thing you can do is start early. Get your tax forms from the post office as soon as they are available and start calculating. This way, if you run into any problems, you have plenty of time to straighten them out. You can also save time by reading the directions carefully. This will prevent time-consuming errors. Finally, if your taxes are relatively simple (you don't have itemized deductions or special investments), use the shorter tax form. It's only one page, so if your records are in order, it can be completed in less than an hour.

2. How many suggestions for tax time does this passage offer?
    a) One.
    b) Two.
    c) Three.
    d) Four.

3. The sentence "It's only one page, so if your records are in order, it can be completed in less than an hour" is:
    a) The main idea of the passage.
    b) A major supporting idea.
    c) A minor supporting idea.
    d) A transitional sentence.

4. A good summary of this passage would be:
    a) Simple strategies can make tax time less taxing.
    b) Don't procrastinate at tax time.
    c) Always keep good records.
    d) Get a tax attorney.

5. According to the passage, who should use the shorter tax form?
   a) Everybody.
   b) People who do not have complicated finances.
   c) People who do have complicated finances.
   d) People who wait until the last minute to file taxes.

6. The sentence, "The single most important strategy is to keep accurate records," is a(n):
   a) Fact.
   b) Opinion.
   c) Both of the above.
   d) Neither of the above.

Being a secretary is a lot like being a parent. After a while, your boss becomes dependent upon you, just as a child is dependent upon his or her parents. Like a child who must ask permission before going out, you'll find your boss coming to you for permission, too. "Can I have a meeting on Tuesday at 3:30?" you might be asked, because you're the one who keeps track of your boss's schedule. You will also find yourself cleaning up after your boss a lot, tidying up papers and files the same way a parent tucks away a child's toys and clothes. And, like a parent protects his or her children from outside dangers, you will find yourself protecting your boss from certain "dangers"—unwanted callers, angry clients, and upset subordinates.

7. The main idea of this passage is:
   a) Secretaries are treated like children.
   b) Bosses treat their secretaries like children.
   c) Secretaries and parents have similar roles.
   d) Bosses depend too much upon their secretaries.

8. Which of the following is the topic sentence of the paragraph?
   a) Being a secretary is a lot like being a parent.
   b) After a while, your boss becomes dependent upon you, just as a child is dependent upon his or her parents.
   c) You will also find yourself cleaning up after your boss a lot, tidying up papers and files the same way a parent tucks away a child's toys and clothes.
   d) None of the above.

9. According to the passage, secretaries are like parents in which of the following ways?
   a) They make their bosses' lives possible.
   b) They keep their bosses from things that might harm or bother them.
   c) They're always cleaning and scrubbing things.
   d) They don't get enough respect.

10. This passage uses which point of view?
   a) First person.
   b) Second person.
   c) Third person.
   d) First and second person.

11. The tone of this passage suggests that:
    a) The writer is angry about how secretaries are treated.
    b) The writer thinks secretaries do too much work.
    c) The writer is slightly amused by how similar the roles of secretaries and parents are.
    d) The writer is both a secretary and a parent.

12. The sentence, "'Can't I have a meeting on Tuesday at 3:30?' you might be asked, because you're the one who keeps track of your boss's schedule," is a:
    a) Main idea.
    b) Major supporting idea.
    c) Minor supporting idea
    d) None of the above.

13. "Being a secretary is a lot like being a parent" is:
    a) A fact.
    b) An opinion.
    c) Neither of the above.
    d) Both of the above.

14. The word "subordinates" probably means:
    a) Employees.
    b) Parents.
    c) Clients.
    d) Secretaries.

Day after day, Johnny chooses to sit at his computer instead of going outside with his friends. A few months ago, he'd get half a dozen phone calls from his friends every night. Now, he might get one or two a week. It used to be that his friends would come over two or three days a week after school. Now, he spends his afternoons alone with his computer.

15. The main idea is:
    a) Johnny and his friends are all spending time with their computers instead of one another.
    b) Johnny's friends aren't very good friends.
    c) Johnny has alienated his friends by spending so much time on the computer.
    d) Johnny and his friends prefer to communicate by computer.

We've had Ginger since I was two years old. Every morning, she wakes me up by licking my cheek. That's her way of telling me she's hungry. When she wants attention, she'll weave in and out of my legs and meow until I pick her up and hold her. And I can always tell when Ginger wants to play. She'll bring me her toys and will keep dropping them (usually right on my homework!) until I stop what I'm doing and play with her for a while.

16. A good topic sentence for this paragraph would be:
    a) I take excellent care of Ginger.
    b) Ginger is a demanding pet.
    c) Ginger and I have grown up together.
    d) Ginger is good at telling me what she wants.

Test Your Knowledge: The Reading Section – Answers

1. c)

2. d)

3. c)

4. a)

5. b)

6. b)

7. c)

8. a)

9. b)

10. b)

11. c)

12. c)

13. b)

14. a)

15. c)

16. d)

Chapter 4: Science

The TEAS will measure your knowledge of the life sciences and physical sciences: Chemistry, Biology, and Physics. Although we can't cover 12 years of schooling – not without a much larger book, anyway! – this section will refresh your memory on the necessary fundamental science principles. Take particular note to the bold faced words. These are the terms most commonly seen on the test.

Here's a breakdown of areas covered:

1. **Biology**
   - Basics of Life
   - Cellular Respiration
   - Classification of Organisms
   - Microorganisms
   - Animals
   - Plants
   - Ecology
   - Cells, Tissues, and Organs
   - Reproduction
   - Heredity
   - The Systems of the Body: Circulatory; Respiratory; Skeletal; Nervous; Muscular; Digestive; Renal

2. **Chemistry**
   - Elements, Compounds, and Mixtures
   - States of Matter
   - The Periodic Table and Chemical Bonds
   - Acids and Bases

3. **Physics**
   - Motion
   - Thermal Physics
   - Heat Transfer
   - Wave Motion (Sound) and Magnetism

Biology

BASICS OF LIFE

We began learning the difference between living (**animate**) beings and nonliving (**inanimate**) objects from an early age. Living organisms and inanimate objects are all composed of **atoms** from elements. Those atoms are arranged into groups called **molecules**, which serve as the building blocks of everything in existence (as we know it). Molecular interactions are what determine whether something is classified as animate or inanimate.   The following is a list of the most commonly-found elements found in the molecules of animate beings:

- Oxygen
- Carbon
- Sodium
- Magnesium
- Iodine
- Sulfur
- Potassium
- Chlorine
- Nitrogen
- Calcium
- Phosphorous
- Iron
- Hydrogen

Another way to describe living and nonliving things is through the terms **organic** and **inorganic.**

- **Organic molecules** are from living organisms. Organic molecules contain **carbon-hydrogen bonds**.

- **Inorganic molecules** come from non-living resources. They do not contain carbon-hydrogen bonds.

There are four major classes of organic molecules:

1. **Carbohydrates**

2. **Lipids**

3. **Proteins**

4. **Nucleic acids**.

Carbohydrates

Carbohydrates consist of only hydrogen, oxygen, and carbon atoms. They are the most abundant single class of organic substances found in nature. Carbohydrate molecules provide many basic necessities such as: fiber, vitamins, and minerals; structural components for organisms, especially plants; and, perhaps most importantly, energy. Our bodies break down carbohydrates to make **glucose**: a sugar used to produce that energy which our bodies need in order to operate. Brain cells are exclusively dependent upon a constant source of glucose molecules.

There are two kinds of carbohydrates: simple and complex.

Simple carbohydrates can be absorbed directly through the cell, and therefore enter the blood stream very quickly. We consume simple carbohydrates in dairy products, fruits, and other sugary foods.

Complex carbohydrates consist of a chain of simple sugars which, over time, our bodies break down into simple sugars (which are also referred to as stored energy.) **Glycogen** is the storage form of glucose in human and animal cells. Complex carbohydrates come from starches like cereal, bread, beans, potatoes, and starchy vegetables.

Lipids

Lipids, commonly known as fats, are molecules with two functions:

1. They are stored as an energy reserve.

2. They provide a protective cushion for vital organs.

In addition to those two functions, lipids also combine with other molecules to form essential compounds, such as **phospholipids,** which form the membranes around cells. Lipids also combine with other molecules to create naturally-occurring **steroid** hormones, like the hormones estrogen and testosterone.

Proteins

Proteins are large molecules which our bodies' cells need in order to function properly. Consisting of **amino acids,** proteins aid in maintaining and creating many aspects of our cells: cellular structure, function, and regulation, to name a few. Proteins also work as neurotransmitters and carriers of oxygen in the blood (hemoglobin).

Without protein, our tissues and organs could not exist. Our muscles bones, skin, and many other parts of the body contain significant amounts of protein. **Enzymes**, hormones, and antibodies are proteins.

Enzymes
When heat is applied, chemical reactions are typically sped up. However, the amount of heat required to speed up reactions could be potentially harmful (even fatal) to living organisms. Instead, our bodies use molecules called enzymes to bring reactants closer together, causing them to form a new compound. Thus, the whole reaction rate is increased without heat. Even better – the enzymes are not consumed during the reaction process, and can therefore be used reused. This makes them an important biochemical part of both photosynthesis and respiration.

Nucleic Acid

Nucleic acids are large molecules made up of smaller molecules called **nucleotides. DNA** (deoxyribonucleic acid) transports and transmits genetic information. As you can tell from the name, DNA is a nucleic acid. Since nucleotides make up nucleic acids, they are considered the basis of reproduction and progression.

Test Your Knowledge: Basics of Life

1. Life depends upon:
   a) The bond energy in molecules.
   b) The energy of protons.
   c) The energy of electrons.
   d) The energy of neutrons.

2. Which of the following elements is **NOT** found in carbohydrates?
   a) Carbon.
   b) Hydrogen.
   c) Oxygen.
   d) Sulfur.

3. Which of the following is a carbohydrate molecule?
   a) Amino acid.
   b) Glycogen.
   c) Sugar.
   d) Lipid.

4. Lipids are commonly known as:
   a) Fat.
   b) Sugar.
   c) Enzymes.
   d) Protein.

5. Proteins are composed of:
   a) Nucleic acids.
   b) Amino acids.
   c) Hormones.
   d) Lipids.

Test Your Knowledge: Basics of Life – Answers

1. a)
2. d)
3. c)
4. a)
5. b)

CELLULAR RESPIRATION

As you can imagine, there are a great deal of processes which require energy: breathing, blood circulation, body temperature control, muscle usage, digestion, brain and nerve functioning are all only a few examples. You can refer to all of the body's physical and chemical processes which convert or use energy as **metabolism**.

All living things in the world, including plants, require energy in order to maintain their metabolisms. Initially, that energy is consumed through food. That energy is processed in plants and animals through **photosynthesis** (for plants) and **respiration** (for animals). **Cellular respiration** produces the actual energy molecules known as **ATP** (Adenosine Tri-Phosphate) molecules.

Plants use ATP during **photosynthesis** for producing glucose, which is then broken down during cellular respiration. This cycle continuously repeats itself throughout the life of the plant.

Photosynthesis: Plants, as well as some Protists and Monerans, can use light energy to bind together small molecules from the environment. These newly-bound molecules are then used as fuel to make more energy. This process is called photosynthesis, and one of its byproducts is none other than oxygen. Most organisms, including plants, require oxygen to fuel the biochemical reactions of metabolism.

You can see in the following equation that plants use the energy taken from light to turn carbon dioxide and water – the small molecules from their environment – into glucose and oxygen.

The photosynthesis equation:

$$CO_2 + H_2O \xrightarrow{\text{Light}} C_6H_{12}O_6 + O_2$$

| Carbon Dioxide | Water | | Glucose (sugar) | Oxygen |

Chlorophyll

In order for photosynthesis to occur, however, plants require a specific molecule to capture sunlight. This molecule is called **chlorophyll**. When chlorophyll absorbs sunlight, one of its electrons is stimulated into a higher energy state. This higher-energy electron then passes that energy onto other electrons in other molecules, creating a chain that eventually results in glucose. Chlorophyll absorbs red and blue light, but not green; green light is reflected off of plants, which is why plants appear green to us. It's important to note that chlorophyll is absolutely necessary to the photosynthesis process in plants –if it photosynthesizes, it will have chlorophyll.

The really fascinating aspect of photosynthesis is that raw sunlight energy is a very nonliving thing; however, it is still absorbed by plants to form the chemical bonds between simple inanimate compounds. This produces organic sugar, which is the chemical basis for the formation of all living compounds. Isn't it amazing? Something nonliving is essential to the creation of all living things!

Respiration

Respiration is the metabolic opposite of photosynthesis. There are two types of respiration: **aerobic** (which uses oxygen) and **anaerobic** (which occurs without the use of oxygen).

You may be confused at thinking of the word "respiration" in this way, since many people use respiration to refer to the process of breathing. However, in biology, breathing is thought of as **inspiration** (inhaling) and **expiration** (exhalation); whereas **respiration** is the metabolic, chemical reaction supporting these processes. Both plants and animals produce carbon dioxide through respiration. **Aerobic respiration** is the reaction which uses enzymes to combine oxygen with organic matter (food). This yields carbon dioxide, water, and energy.

The respiration equation looks like this:

$$\overset{\textbf{Enzymes}}{C6H12O6 + 6O2 \longrightarrow 7\ 6CO2 + 6H2O + energy}$$

If you look back the equation for photosynthesis, you will see that respiration is almost the same equation, only it goes in the opposite direction. (Photosynthesis uses carbon dioxide and water, with the help of energy, to create oxygen and glucose. Respiration uses oxygen and glucose, with the help of enzymes, to create carbon dioxide, water, and energy.)

Anaerobic respiration is respiration that occurs WITHOUT the use of oxygen. It produces less energy than aerobic respiration produces, yielding only two molecules of ATP per glucose molecule Aerobic respiration produces 38 ATP per glucose molecule.

So, plants convert energy into matter and release oxygen gas – animals then absorb this oxygen gas in order to run their own metabolic reaction and, in the process, release carbon dioxide. That carbon dioxide is then absorbed by plants in the photosynthetic conversion of energy into matter. Everything comes full circle! This is called a **metabolic cycle.**

Test Your Knowledge: Cellular Respiration

1. Which of the following is **NOT** true of enzymes?
   a) Enzymes are lipid molecules.
   b) Enzymes are not consumed in a biochemical reaction.
   c) Enzymes are important in photosynthesis and respiration.
   d) Enzymes speed up reactions and make them more efficient.

2. Plants appear green because chlorophyll:
   a) Absorbs green light.
   b) Reflects red light.
   c) Absorbs blue light.
   d) Reflects green light.

3. Photosynthesis is the opposite of:
   a) Enzymatic hydrolysis.
   b) Protein synthesis.
   c) Respiration.
   d) Reproduction.

4. The compound that absorbs light energy during photosynthesis is:
   a) Chloroform.
   b) Chlorofluorocarbon.
   c) Chlorinated biphenyls.
   d) Chlorophyll.

5. What is the name of the sugar molecule produced during photosynthesis?
   a) Chlorophyll.
   b) Glycogen.
   c) Glucose.
   d) Fructose.

Test Your Knowledge: Cellular Respiration – Answers

1. **a)**
2. **d)**
3. **c)**
4. **d)**
5. **c)**

CLASSIFICATION OF ORGANISMS

All of Earth's organisms have characteristics which distinguish them from one another. Scientists have developed systems to organize and classify all of Earth's organisms based on those characteristics.

Kingdoms

Through the process of evolution, organisms on Earth have developed into many diverse forms, which have complex relationships. Scientists have organized life into five large groups called **kingdoms**. Each kingdom contains those organisms that share significant characteristics distinguishing them from organisms in other kingdoms. These five kingdoms are named as follows:

1. **Animalia**

2. **Plantae**

3. **Fungi**

4. **Protista**

5. **Monera**

Kingdom Animalia

This kingdom contains multicellular organisms multicellular, or those known as complex organisms. These organisms are generically called **heterotrophs**, which means that they must eat preexisting organic matter (either plants or other animals) in order to sustain themselves.

Those heterotrophs which eat only plants are called **herbivores** (from "herbo," meaning "herb" or "plant"); those that kill and eat other animals for food are called **carnivores** (from "carno," meaning "flesh" or "meat"); and still other animals eat both plants *and* other animals – they are called **omnivores** (from "omnis," which means "all").

Those organisms in the Animal Kingdom have nervous tissue which has developed into nervous systems and brains; they are also able to move from place to place using muscular systems. The Animal Kingdom is divided into two groups: **vertebrates** (with backbones) and **invertebrates** (without backbones).

Kingdom Plantae

As you can guess from its name, the Plant Kingdom contains all plant-based life. Plants are multicellular organisms that use chlorophyll, which is held in specialized cellular structures called **chloroplasts,** to capture sunlight energy. Remember: photosynthesis! They then convert that sunlight energy into organic matter: their food. Because of this, most plants are referred to as **autotrophs** (self-feeders). There are a few organisms included in the Plant Kingdom which are not multicellular – certain types of algae which, while not multicellular, have cells with a nucleus. These algae also contain chlorophyll.

Except for algae, most plants are divided into one of two groups: **vascular plants** (most crops, trees, and flowering plants) and **nonvascular plants** (mosses). Vascular plants have specialized tissue that allows them to transport water and nutrients from their roots, to their leaves, and back again – even when the plant is several hundred feet tall. Nonvascular plants cannot do this, and therefore remain very small in size. Vascular plants are able to grow in both wet and dry environments; whereas nonvascular plants, since they are unable to transport water, are usually found only in wet, marshy areas.

Kingdom Fungi

The Fungi Kingdom contains organisms that share some similarities with plants, but also have other characteristics that make them more animal-like. For example, they resemble animals in that they lack chlorophyll – so they can't perform photosynthesis. This means that they don't produce their own food and are therefore heterotrophs.

However, they resemble plants in that they reproduce by spores; they also resemble plants in appearance. The bodies of fungi are made of filaments called **hyphae**, which in turn create the tissue **mycelium.** The most well-known examples of organisms in this Kingdom are mushrooms, yeasts, and molds. Fungi are very common and benefit other organisms, including humans.

Kingdom Protista

This kingdom includes single-celled organisms that contain a nucleus as part of their structure. They are considered a simple cell, but still contain multiple structures and accomplish many functions. This Kingdom includes organisms such as paramecium, amoeba, and slime molds. They often move around using hair-like structures called *cilia* or *flagellums.*

Kingdom Monera

This kingdom contains only bacteria. All of these organisms are single-celled and do not have a nucleus. They have only one chromosome, which is used to transfer genetic information. Sometimes they can also transmit genetic information using small structures called **plasmids.** Like organisms in the Protista Kingdom, they use flagella to move. Bacteria usually reproduce asexually.

There are more forms of bacteria than any other organism on Earth. Some bacteria are beneficial to us, like the ones found in yogurt; others can cause us to get sick such as the bacteria *E. coli.*

KINGDOM	DESCRIPTION	EXAMPLES
Animalia	Multi-celled; parasites; prey; consumers; can be herbivorous, carnivorous, or omnivorous	Sponges, worms, insects, fish, mammals, reptiles, birds, humans
Plantae	Multi-celled; autotrophs; mostly producers	Ferns, angiosperms, gymnosperms, mosses
Fungi	Can be single or multi-celled; decomposers; parasites; absorb food; asexual; consumers	Mushrooms, mildew, molds, yeast
Protista	Single or multi-celled; absorb food; both producers and consumers	Plankton, algae, amoeba, protozoans
Monera	Single-celled or a colony of single-cells; decomposers and parasites; move in water; are both producers and consumers	Bacteria, blue-green algae

Levels of Classification

Kingdom groupings are not very specific. They contain organisms defined by broad characteristics, and which may not seem similar at all. For example, worms belong in Kingdom Animalia – but then, so do birds. These two organisms are very different, despite sharing the necessary traits to make it into the animal kingdom. Therefore, to further distinguish different organisms, we have multiple levels of classification, which gradually become more specific until we finally reach the actual organism.

We generally start out by grouping organisms into the appropriate kingdom. Within each kingdom, we have other subdivisions: **Phylum, Class, Order, Family, Genus, and Species.** (In some cases, "Species" can be further narrowed down into "Sub-Species.")

As we move down the chain, characteristics become more specific, and the number of organisms in each group decreases. For an example, let's try to classify a grizzly bear. The chart would go as follows:

Kingdom - insect, fish, bird, pig, dog, bear

Phylum - fish, bird, pig, dog, bear

Class - pig, dog, bear

Order - dog, bear

Family - panda, brown, grizzly

Genus - brown, grizzly

Species - grizzly

Here is an easy way to remember the order of terms used in this classification scheme:

Kings Play Cards On Friday, Generally Speaking.

Kingdom, **P**hylum, **C**lass, **O**rder, **F**amily, **G**enus, **S**pecies

Binomial Nomenclature

Organisms can be positively identified by two Latin words. Therefore, the organism naming system is referred to as a binomial nomenclature ("binomial" referring to the number two, and "nomenclature" referring to a title or name). Previously-used words help illustrate where the organism fits into the whole scheme, but it is only the last two, the genus and species, that specifically name an organism. Both are written in italics. The genus is always capitalized, but the species name is written lowercase.

Grizzly bears fall underneath the genus *Ursus*, species *arctos*, and sub-species *horribilis*. Therefore, the scientific name of the grizzly bear would be *Ursus arctos horribilis*. *Canis familiaris* is the scientific name for a common dog, *Felis domesticus* is a common cat, and humans are *Homo sapiens*.

Test Your Knowledge: Classification of Organisms

1. Which feature distinguishes those organisms in Kingdom Monera from those in other kingdoms? Organisms in Kingdom Monera:
   a) Contain specialized organelles.
   b) Contain a nucleus.
   c) Contain chloroplasts.
   d) Lack a nucleus.

2. Which of the following has the classification levels in the correct order, from most general to most specific?
   a) Kingdom, Phylum, Class, Order, Family, Genus, Species.
   b) Order, Family, Genus, Species, Class, Phylum, Kingdom.
   c) Species, Genus, Family, Order, Class, Phylum, Kingdom.
   d) Kingdom, Phylum, Class, Species, Genus, Family, Order.

3. The _____ contains organisms with both plant-and-animal-like characteristics?
   a) Animal Kingdom.
   b) Plant Kingdom.
   c) Fungi Kingdom.
   d) Monera Kingdom.

4. Which of the following statements is true about the binomial nomenclature system of classification?
   a) The genus and species names describe a specific organism.
   b) The category of kingdom is very specific.
   c) The category of species is very broad.
   d) Three names are needed to correctly specify a particular organism.

5. Which of the following kingdom's members are multicellular AND autotrophic?
   a) Fungi.
   b) Animalia.
   c) Protista.
   d) Plantae.

6. Which of the following kingdom's members have tissue called hyphae?
   a) Fungi.
   b) Animalia.
   c) Protista.
   d) Plantae.

Test Your Knowledge: Classification of Organisms – Answers

1. **d)**

2. **a)**

3. **c)**

4. **a)**

5. **d)**

6. **a)**

MICROORGANISMS

Microorganisms (microbes) are extremely small and cannot be seen with the naked eye. They can be detected using either a microscope or through various chemical tests. These organisms are everywhere, even in such extreme environments as very hot areas, very cold areas, dry areas, and deep in the ocean under tremendous pressure. Some of these organisms cause diseases in animals, plants, and humans. However, most are helpful to us and the Earth's ecosystems. In fact, we are totally dependent upon microbes for our quality of life. There are three types of microorganisms: **bacteria, protists, and fungi.**

Bacteria

Bacteria are microorganisms that do not have a true nucleus; their genetic material simply floats around in the cell. They are very small, simple, one-celled organisms. Bacteria are normally found in three variations: **bacilli** (rod-shaped), **cocci** (sphere-shaped), and **spirilla** (spiral-shaped). Bacteria are widespread in all environments and are important participants within all ecosystems. They are **decomposers**, because they break down dead organic matter into basic molecules.

Bacteria are also an important part of the food-chain, because they are eaten by other organisms. Still, bacteria remain the most numerous organisms on Earth. This is due to the fact that they are small, can live practically anywhere, and have great metabolic flexibility. But most importantly, bacteria have the ability to rapidly reproduce. In the right environment, any bacteria can reproduce every 20 or 30 minutes, each one doubling after each reproduction.

> **Benefits of Bacteria** – Some bacteria are found in our intestinal tracts, where they help to digest our food and make vitamins.

> To demonstrate the significance of bacteria, let's look at the cycle of nitrogen, which is used by organisms to make proteins. The cycle starts with dead plants being decomposed by bacteria. The nitrogen from the plant tissue is released into the atmosphere, where nitrifying bacteria convert that nitrogen into ammonia-type compounds. Other bacteria act upon these compounds to form nitrates for plants to absorb. When these new plants die, we are brought back again to the decomposing bacteria releasing the plant's nitrogen into the atmosphere.

> **Bacterial Diseases** - Microorganisms, including bacteria, enter our bodies in a variety of ways: through the air we breathe, ingestion by mouth, or through the skin via a cut or injury. We can eliminate much of this threat by disinfecting utensils and thoroughly washing our hands. This destroys bacteria and other microorganisms which may cause disease.

Protists

Protists are very diversified and include organisms that range greatly in size – from single cells to considerably complex structures, some longer than 100 meters. Protists have a wide variety of reproductive and nutritional strategies, and their genetic material is enclosed within a nucleus. Even

121

though protists are more simplistic than other organisms with cellular nuclei, they are not as primitive as bacteria.

Some are autotrophic and contain chlorophyll; others are heterotrophic and consume other organisms to survive. Because protists obtain food in both of these ways, it is generally believed that early protists were both animal- and plant-like. Protists are important to food chains and ecosystems, although some protists do cause disease.

Fungi

Fungi are heterotrophic and can be either single-celled or multi-celled. They play an important decomposition role in an ecosystem, because they consume dead organic matter. This returns nutrients to the soil for eventual uptake by plants.

There are three types of fungi which obtain food: saprophytic, parasitic, and mycorrhizal-associated.

Saprophytic fungi consume dead organic matter; **parasitic** fungi attack living plants and animals; and **mycorrhizal-associated** fungi form close relationships (**symbiosis**) with trees, shrubs, and other plants, where each partner in the relationship mutually benefits. An organism called **lichen** is an example of a symbiotic union between a fungus and algae.

Fungi produce **spores** (reproductive structures) that are highly resistant to extreme temperatures and moisture levels. This gives them the ability to survive for a long time, even in aggressive environments. When their environments become more favorable, the spores **germinate** (sprout) and grow. Spores are able to travel to new areas, which spreads the organism. Fungi absorb food through **hyphae**. A large mass of joined, branched hyphae is called the **mycelium**, which constitutes the main body of the multicellular fungi. However, the mycelium is not usually seen, because it is hidden throughout the food source which is being consumed. The largest organism in the world is believed to be a soil fungus whose mycelium tissue extends for many acres!

What we do usually see of a fungus is the fungal fruiting body. A mushroom is a fruiting body filled with spores. The main body of the mushroom (the **mycelium**) is under the soil surface.

Test Your Knowledge: Microorganisms

1. Fungi are decomposers, which is important for_____.
   a) Making nutrients available for recycling back into the soil.
   b) Producing oxygen by photosynthesizing.
   c) Producing oxygen by respiration.
   d) Living in mostly aquatic environments.

2. Which is the most numerous organism on Earth?
   a) Paramecium from the Protist Kingdom.
   b) Yeast from the Fungi Kingdom.
   c) Euglena from the Protist Kingdom.
   d) Bacteria from the Moneran Kingdom.

3. Which kingdom contains organisms that are able to convert atmospheric nitrogen to nitrate?
   a) Animalia.
   b) Plantae.
   c) Monera.
   d) Protista.

4. Why are spores produced?
   a) They are part of resistance.
   b) To reproduce.
   c) To photosynthesize.
   d) They are part of the support system.

5. Members of the Kingdom Monera are found in our digestive tracts and perform which of the following functions?
   a) Produce carbohydrates.
   b) Produce vitamins.
   c) Produce lipids.
   d) Produce proteins.

Test Your Knowledge: Microorganisms – Answers

1. **a)**
2. **d)**
3. **c)**
4. **b)**
5. **b)**

ANIMALS

Animals are multi-celled and unable to produce their own food internally, just like plants. As mentioned previously, the Animal Kingdom is divided into two large groupings: the **invertebrates** and **vertebrates.**

Invertebrates are multicellular, have no back bone or cell walls, reproduce sexually, and are heterotrophic. They make up approximately 97% of the animal population.

Vertebrates, on the other hand, have well-developed internal skeletons, highly developed brains, an advanced nervous system, and an outer covering of protective cellular skin. They make up the remaining 3% of the animals.

What Is an Animal?

All animals, from sponges to human beings, share some fundamental characteristics. One such characteristic is cellular division. At the beginning of reproduction, an egg is fertilized and then undergoes several cell divisions (cleavages); this process quickly produces a cluster of cells. Cell division continues through many distinct stages before finally resulting in an embryo. The full, multi-celled organism then develops tissues and organ systems, eventually developing into its adult form.

All multicellular animals must come up with solutions to several basic problems:

- **Surface-area-to-volume issues:** Nutrients, air, and water must be able to enter an animal's body in order to sustain life; therefore, the surface area of an animal's body must be large enough to allow a sufficient amount of these elements to be consumed by the organism. In single-celled organisms, the cell size is limited to the amount of nutrients able to pass through the cell membrane to support the cell. In multi-celled organisms, specialized tissues and organ systems with very large surface areas bring in the necessary elements and then carry them to the cells. Those specialized tissues are found in the respiratory system, urinary system, excretory system, and the digestive system. These tissues and organs, along with the circulatory system, are able to support a large-sized body.

- **Body support and protection:** All animals have some form of support and protection in the form of their internal or external skeletal systems. These skeletal systems provide support for the animal's body and protect the internal organs from damage.

- **Mobility:** Animals are heterotrophs and must acquire food; this need, along with the need to mate and reproduce, requires the animal to move. Although plants move, they are considered stationary because they are rooted. Animals, on the other hand, move from place to place; this is called **locomotion.** Locomotion requires a muscular system. Muscles are found only in animals; they are not present in plants, fungi, or single-celled microorganisms.

- **Sensory integration**: Animals have many specialized sensory organs: eyes, ears, noses, etc. These organs make animals aware of the environment and give them the ability to respond to environmental stimuli. The integration and coordination of sense organs with other bodily functions requires an organized collection of specialized nervous tissue, known as a **central nervous system** (CNS).

A Few Animal Phyla

Phylum Porifera: Sponges.
Collections of individual cells with no tissues or organs, and no nervous system or skeleton.

Phylum Coelenterata: Jellyfish, sea anemones, and coral.
Bodies symmetrical in a circular fashion with rudimentary organs and systems, but no skeleton.

Phylum Echinodermata: Sea stars and sea urchins.
Bodies have circular symmetry with five body parts arranged around a central axis. They have calcium spines or plates just under the skin.

Phylum Mollusca: Snails, clams, and octopi.
These have a well-developed circulatory system, nervous system, and digestive system; octopuses have particularly well-developed brains.

Phylum Arthropoda: Crustaceans, spiders, and insects.
This phylum has more species than the other phyla. They have exoskeletons, and most undergo **metamorphosis** (a physical transformation that is a part of the growth process). They often have specialized body parts (antennae, pinchers, etc.), and they are well adapted to many environments.

Phylum Chordata: Amphibians, reptiles, fish, birds, and mammals (including humans).
All share four characteristics: a notochord that develops into the vertebral column in vertebrates, a nerve cord that runs along the spinal column, gill slits at some point in our development, and a tail or at least a vestigial tail (humans have the tailbone or coccyx).

Test Your Knowledge: Animals

1. Multicellular animals have developed respiratory and excretory systems to overcome which of the following issues?
   a) Weight versus mass.
   b) Surface-area-to-volume.
   c) Height to weight.
   d) Mass to volume.

2. The two categories of animals are:
   a) Single-celled and multi-celled.
   b) Autotrophic and heterotrophic.
   c) Those that live in water and those that live on land.
   d) Vertebrate and invertebrate.

3. Jellyfish and coral are related to:
   a) Octopi.
   b) Sea anemones.
   c) Sea urchins.
   d) Sponges.

4. The Phylum Arthropoda contains which of the following animals?
   a) Spiders.
   b) Sea stars.
   c) Sponges.
   d) Seals.

5. Humans are classified under which of the following Phyla?
   a) Echinodermata.
   b) Chordata.
   c) Mollusca.
   d) Platyhelminthes.

Test Your Knowledge: Animals – Answers

1. **b)**
2. **d)**
3. **b)**
4. **a)**
5. **b)**

PLANTS

Organisms within Kingdom Plantae are very diverse, but they usually share certain characteristics which make them recognizable as plants. Chlorophyll ensures that some, if not all, of a plants body will have a green color, and their root systems render plants incapable of locomotion. Remember photosynthesis? Plants are autotrophs; they create their own food through photosynthesis, which turns carbon dioxide and water into sugars and oxygen gas. This process takes place using chlorophyll in structures called **chloroplasts**. Plants also have hard cell walls made of the carbohydrate **cellulose**.

Diverse Environments and Plants

Plants are found in nearly every place on Earth. Since plants need light to photosynthesize, their ability to survive in different environments depends upon their access to sources of light. Water is also an important part of a plant's growth and development, partly because the water contained within a plant cells (by the cell wall) provide a plant with structure and support.

Land plants evolved from algae into two large groups: **bryophytes** (nonvascular plants) and **tracheophytes** (vascular plants).

Bryophytes
Quite different from tracheophytes, bryophytes lack roots, leaves, and stems. Instead, structures called **rhizoids** (root-like hairs) absorb water and nutrients. Since they do not have a tubular system with which to move water throughout their bodies, bryophytes rely on diffusion to distribute water and nutrients. This process is slow, and not efficient enough to support large bodies, so bryophytes cannot grow very large. The largest types of bryophytes are liverworts and mosses.

Tracheophytes
These plants have tubes (vessels) which provide both support and a means of transporting water and nutrients throughout their bodies. This support enables them to grow much larger than bryophytes.

The tracheophyte group is further broken down into two types: **seedless** and **seeded** vascular plants.

> **Seedless** vascular plants require moist environments, because they need water to reproduce. Millions of years ago, seedless plants dominated the Earth; you can see many of them still today, such as club mosses, horsetails, and ferns.

> **Seeded** vascular plants have become dominant today because they have developed a reproductive system that includes pollen and seeds. In response to harsh and dangerous conditions, plants have developed **pollen** as a structure to protect sperm cells until they can safely reach the female part of a flower. Another structure which protects plants against the environment is a seed. **Seeds** contain and protect an immature plant in a state of dormancy until conditions are favorable. They then germinate and form a new plant.

> Since plants cannot transport themselves (remember: no locomotion), they depend on dispersal systems to establish themselves in new areas. Many systems help distribute seeds, including wind, water, and animals.

127

Seeded vascular plants are divided into two groups: **gymnosperms** and **angiosperms**.

Gymnosperms are seeded vascular plants that do not flower. They include plants such as pines, spruce, and cypresses. Gymnosperms are adapted to cold dry areas. They have very thin, small leaves covered with a waterproof layer that keeps them from drying out; additionally, a biological antifreeze in their sap keeps them from freezing. Gymnosperms retain green leaves year-round and produce seeds in cones.

Angiosperms are seeded vascular plants that *do* form flowers. These plants have thrived. They dominate the Earth and are highly diverse, largely because they have developed flowers, fruits, and broad leaves.

Broad leaves capture more sunlight, and therefore produce more food than the narrow, thin leaves of the gymnosperms are able to produce.

Flowers are the place in plants where sperm and egg cells are produced – they contain both the male and female sexual parts. A flower is designed to attract animals, which is why their structures are so colorful and fragrant. Animals assist in the pollination process by carrying pollen and other seeds to diverse locations; the animal often receives a "reward" from the plant in the form of nectar or pollen. Bees, for example, receive nectar and pollen for food from flowering plants.

Fruits contain the fully developed seed of flowering seed plants. Animals are attracted to the plant, eat the fruit, and then disperse the seeds.

Test Your Knowledge: Plants

1. Which of the following characteristics is NOT a characteristic of plants?
   a) They are able to engage in locomotion by moving from place to place.
   b) They use chlorophyll contained in chloroplasts.
   c) They produce sugars and oxygen.
   d) They use carbon dioxide and water in photosynthesis.

2. Which of the following is a bryophyte?
   a) Horsetail.
   b) Fern.
   c) Liverwort.
   d) Spruce tree.

3. Which plant group currently dominates the Earth in terms of quantity over other plant groups?
   a) Gymnosperms.
   b) Bryophytes.
   c) Seedless vascular plants.
   d) Angiosperms.

4. "Tracheophytes" is another name for:
   a) Nonvascular plants.
   b) Angiosperm plants.
   c) Gymnosperm plants.
   d) Vascular plants.

5. Which of the following strategies does an angiosperm plant NOT use to attract animals?
   a) It produces pollen.
   b) It produces nectar.
   c) It produces chloroplasts.
   d) It produces fruit.

6. Rhizoids are similar to _____ in vascular plants?
   a) Leaves
   b) Chloroplasts
   c) Roots
   d) Stems

Test Your Knowledge: Plants – Answers

1. a)
2. c)
3. d)
4. d)
5. c)
6. c)

ECOLOGY

Biosphere and Biome

Life is possible due to the presence of air (**atmosphere**), water (**hydrosphere**), and soil (**lithosphere**). These factors interact with each other and the life on Earth to create an environment called a **biosphere**. The biosphere contains all of Earth's living organisms. Smaller living systems called **biomes** exist in large areas, both on land and in water; they are defined by the physical characteristics of the environment which they encompass, and by the organisms living within it.

Ecosystem

An ecosystem is a community of living and non-living things that work together. Ecosystems have no particular size; from large lakes and deserts, to small trees or puddles. Everything in the natural world – water, water temperature, plants, animals, air, light, soil, etc. – all form ecosystems.

The physical environment of an ecosystem includes soils, weather, climate, the topography (or shape) of the land, and many other factors. If there isn't enough light or water within an ecosystem, or if the soil doesn't have the right nutrients, plants will die. If plants die, the animals which depend on them will die. If the animals depending upon the plants die, any other animals depending upon those animals will also die. Regardless of the type of ecosystem they are in, all organisms – even microscopic ones – are affected by each other and their physical surroundings.

There are two components of an ecosystem. The **biotic** (biological) component includes the living organisms; nonliving factors – such as water, minerals, and sunlight – are collectively known as the **abiotic** (non-biological) component. While all ecosystems have different organisms and/or abiotic factors, they all have two primary features:

1. **Energy flows in one direction**. Beginning in the form of chemical bonds from photosynthetic organisms, like green plants or algae, energy flows first to the animals that eat the plants, then to other animals.

2. **Inorganic materials are recycled.** When taken up from the environment through living organisms, inorganic minerals are returned to the environment – mainly via decomposers such as bacteria and fungi. Other organisms called **detritivores** (such as pill bugs, sow bugs, millipedes, and earthworms), help break down large pieces of organic matter into smaller pieces that are handled then by the decomposers.

But since that's a lot of information to take in at once, here's a simple and complete definition of an ecosystem: a combination of biotic and abiotic components, through which energy flows and inorganic material is recycled.

An Organism's Niche

The area in which an organism lives – and therefore acquires the many things needed to sustain their lives – is called a **habitat.** An organism's role within its community, how it affects its habitat and how it is affected by its habitat, are the factors that define the organism's **niche.** A niche is like an organism's "location" and "occupation" within a community. For example, birds and squirrels both live in a tree habitat; however, they eat different foods, have different living arrangements, and have different food-gathering abilities. Therefore, the do not occupy the same niche.

THE ECOLOGICALORDER OF LIFE

Biosphere - All ecosystems on the planet make up the biosphere.

Ecosystem – Large community of numerous communities, and the physical non-living environment.

Community - A group of populations in a given area.

Population - A group of organisms of the same species in a given area.

Organism - A living thing.

Organ Systems - A group of organs that perform certain functions to form an organism.

Organs - A group of tissues that perform a certain function to form organ systems.

Tissues - A group of cells that perform certain functions to form an organ.

Cells - The building blocks of life which form tissues.

Organelles - Small parts of cells that have specific functions.

Atoms and Molecules - the building blocks of everything in the universe as we know it

---

One of the most important relationships among organisms exists between predators and their prey. You may have heard of this relationship described through **food chains** and **food webs**.

Food Chains represent the flow of energy obtained from the chemical breakdown of food molecules. When one animal (the predator) consumes another (the prey), the chemical bonds making up the tissues of the prey's body are broken down by the predator's digestive system. This digestive process releases energy and smaller chemical molecules that the predator's body uses to make more tissue. Prior to being the consumed, the prey obtains energy from foods for its own life processes.

Here's a basic example of a food chain:

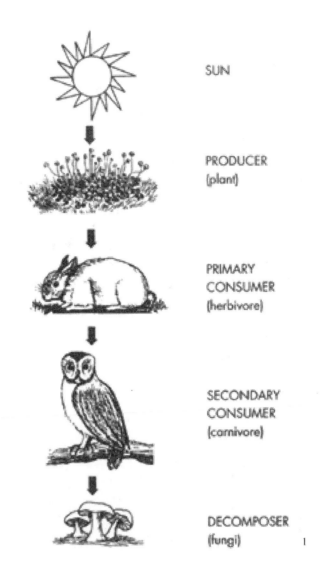

SUN

PRODUCER
(plant)

PRIMARY
CONSUMER
(herbivore)

SECONDARY
CONSUMER
(carnivore)

DECOMPOSER
(fungi)

Food chains are a part of **food webs**, which offer a more complex view of energy transfer. They include more organisms, taking into account more than one predator-prey relationship. Each step along a food chain, or within a food web, is called a **trophic** (or feeding) level. Organisms at that first trophic level are known as **primary producers**, and are always photosynthetic organisms, whether on land or in water.

At the second trophic level, herbivores (referred to as **primary consumers**) eat plants to produce the energy needed for their metabolism. Much of the energy that transfers from the first trophic level to the second level is not turned into tissue. Instead, it is used for the digestive process, locomotion, and is lost as heat. As you move from one trophic level to another, it is estimated that only 10% of the available energy gets turned into body tissue at the next level up.

[1] Graphic from: http://www.king.portlandschools.org

The following is an example of a food web:

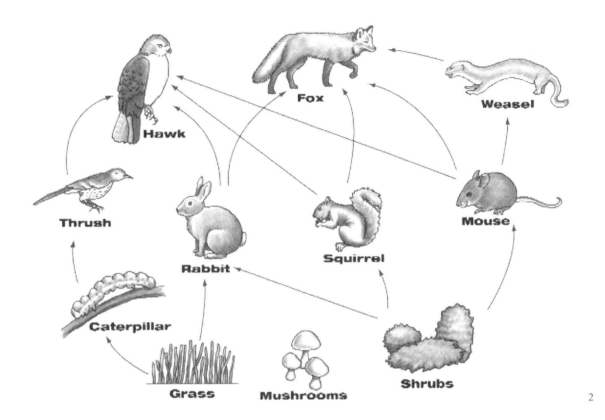

Test Your Knowledge: Ecology

1. Ecology is the study of organisms interacting with:
   a) The physical environment only.
   b) The internal environment only.
   c) The physical environment and each other.
   d) Each other and the internal environment.

2. In terms of energy, an ecosystem is defined as:
   a) Moving energy back and forth between organisms.
   b) Moving energy in one direction from plants to animals.
   c) Not utilizing energy.
   d) Moving energy in one direction from animals to plants.

3. Decomposers are important because they:
   a) Recycle nutrients.
   b) Produce sugars.
   c) Produce oxygen.
   d) Engage in asexual reproduction.

4. Which of the following best describes the concept of an organism's niche?
   a) It is the organism's function, or "occupation", within an ecosystem.
   b) It is the organism's location, or "address", within an ecosystem.
   c) It is both an organism's function and location in an ecosystem.
   d) It is the binomial classification of an organism in an ecosystem.

5. Pillbugs are also known as:
   a) Decomposers.
   b) Detritivores.
   c) Producers.
   d) Autotrophs.

6. The steps in a food chain or food web are called _____ and represent the _____ of an organism.
   a) biome levels; energy level
   b) trophic levels; energy level
   c) trophic levels; feeding level
   d) energy levels; feeding level

7. Another term for herbivores is:
   a) Plants.
   b) Secondary consumers.
   c) Primary consumers
   d) Third trophic-level organisms.

8. Several interacting food chains form a:
   a) Food pyramid.
   b) Food web.
   c) Food column.
   d) Food triangle.

9. Herbivores are at the second trophic level, so they are:
  a) Primary producers.
  b) Primary consumers.
  c) Secondary consumers.
  d) Secondary producers.

Test Your Knowledge: Ecology – Answers

1. c)
2. b)
3. a)
4. c)
5. b)
6. c)
7. c)
8. b)
9. b)

CELLS, TISSUES, AND ORGANS

All organisms are composed of microscopic cells, although the type and number of cells may vary. A cell is the minimum amount of organized living matter that is complex enough to carry out the functions of life. This section will briefly review both animal and plant cells, noting their basic similarities and differences.

Cell Structure

Around the cell is the **cell membrane**, which separates the living cell from the rest of the environment and regulates the comings and goings of molecules within the cell. Because the cell membrane allows some molecules to pass through while blocking others, it is considered **semipermeable.** Each cell's membrane communicates and interacts with the membranes of other cells. In additional to a cell membrane, *plants* also have a **cell wall** which is necessary for structural support and protection. Animal cells do not contain a cell wall.

Organelle

Cells are filled with a gelatin-like substance called **protoplasm** which contains various structures called **organelles**; called so because they act like small versions of organs. The diagram on the next page illustrates the basic organelles of both a plant and an animal cell. Pay attention to the differences and similarities between the two.

Mitochondrion
Nucleus (surrounded by nuclear membrane)
Microtubules ("tiny tubes")
Cell wall (rigid)
Plasma (cell) membrane
Rough ER (studded with ribosomes)
Smooth ER (no attached ribosomes)
Microfilaments ("tiny threads")
Central vacuole
Golgi body
Chloroplast (filled with chlorophyll)

(A)

3

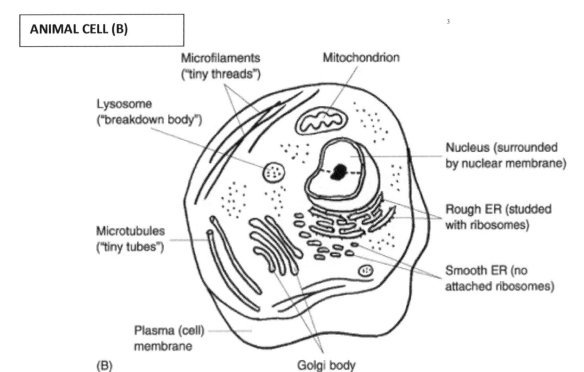

Microfilaments ("tiny threads")
Mitochondrion
Lysosome ("breakdown body")
Nucleus (surrounded by nuclear membrane)
Rough ER (studded with ribosomes)
Microtubules ("tiny tubes")
Smooth ER (no attached ribosomes)
Plasma (cell) membrane
Golgi body

(B)

---

3 Graphics from: http://www.education.com

Organelles (Defined)

Mitochondria are spherical or rod-shaped organelles which carry out the reactions of aerobic respiration. They are the power generators of both plant and animal cells, because they convert oxygen and nutrients into ATP, the chemical energy that powers the cell's metabolic activities.

Ribosomes are extremely tiny spheres that make proteins. These proteins are used either as enzymes or as support for other cell functions.

The **Golgi Apparatus** is essential to the production of polysaccharides (carbohydrates), and made up of a layered stack of flattened sacs.

The **Endoplasmic Reticulum** is important in the synthesis and packaging of proteins. It is a complex system of internal membranes, and is called either rough (when ribosomes are attached), or smooth (no ribosomes attached).

Chloroplasts are only found in plants. They contain the chlorophyll molecule necessary for photosynthesis.

The **Nucleus** controls all of the cell's functions, and contains the all-important genetic information, or DNA, of a cell.

Cellular Differentiation

Single-celled organisms have only one cell to carry out all of their required biochemical and structural functions. On the other hand, multi-celled organisms – except for very primitive ones (i.e. sponges) – have various groups of cells called **tissues** that each perform specific functions (**differentiation**).

There are four main types of tissues: **epithelial**, **connective, muscular,** and **nervous**.

Epithelial tissue is made up groups of flattened cells which are grouped tightly together to form a solid surface. Those cells are arranged in one or many layer(s) to form an external or internal covering of the body or organs. Epithelial tissue protects the body from injury and allows for the exchange of gases in the lungs and bronchial tubes. There's even a form of epithelial tissue that produces eggs and sperm, an organism's sex cells.

Connective tissue is made of cells which are surrounded by non-cellular material. For example, bones contain some cells, but they are also surrounded by a considerable amount of non-cellular, extracellular material.

Muscular tissue has the ability to contract. There are three types:

1. **Cardiac** tissue, found in the heart.

2. **Smooth** tissue, located in the walls of hollow internal structures such as blood vessels, the stomach, intestines, and urinary bladder.

3. **Skeletal** (or striated) tissue, found in the muscles.

Nervous tissue consists of cells called **neurons.** Neurons specialize in making many connections with and transmitting electrical impulses to each other. The brain, spinal cord, and peripheral nerves are all made of nervous tissue.

Organs and Organ Systems

As living organisms go through their life cycle, they grow and/or develop. Single-celled organisms grow and develop very rapidly; whereas complex, multi-celled organisms take much longer to progress. All organisms go through changes as they age. These changes involve the development of more complex functions, which in turn require groups of tissues to form larger units called **organs.** Here are some examples of organs:

1. **The heart** - Made of cardiac muscle and conjunctive tissue (conjunctive tissue makes up the valves), the heart pumps blood first to the lungs in order to pick up oxygen, then through the rest of the body to deliver the oxygen, and finally back to the lungs to start again.

2. **Roots** - A tree's are covered by an epidermis which is in turn made up of a protective tissue. They are also *composed* of tissue, which allows them to grow. The root organ also contains **conductive tissue** to absorb and transport water and nutrients to the rest of the plant.

Generally, in complex organisms like plants and animals, many organs are grouped together into **systems.** For example, many combinations of tissues make up the many organs which create the digestive system in animals. The organs in the digestive system consist of the mouth, the esophagus, the stomach, small and large intestines, the liver, the pancreas, and the gall bladder.

Test Your Knowledge: Cells, Tissues, and Organs

1. Which statement is true about Earth's organisms?
   a) All organisms are based on the cell as the basic unit of life.
   b) Protists are an exception to the cell theory and are not based on cells.
   c) Only single-celled organisms are based on cells.
   d) All organisms are based on tissues as the basic unit of life.

2. What organelle produces the cell's energy source?
   a) Chloroplast.
   b) Nucleus.
   c) Mitochondrion.
   d) Endoplasmic reticulum.

3. The formation of tissue depends upon:
   a) Cell differentiation.
   b) Cell membranes.
   c) Cell death.
   d) Cell organelles.

4. Cardiac muscle is an example of what tissue?
   a) Smooth muscle.
   b) Nervous.
   c) Contractile.
   d) Connective.

5. Which organelle has two forms: rough and smooth?
   a) Mitochondrion.
   b) Golgi apparatus.
   c) Nucleus.
   d) Endoplasmic reticulum.

6. Which organelle is important in the production of polysaccharides (carbohydrates)?
   a) Mitochondrion.
   b) Golgi apparatus.
   c) Nucleus
   d) Endoplasmic reticulum.

Test Your Knowledge: Cells, Tissues, and Organs – Answers

1. **a)**
2. **c)**
3. **a)**
4. **c)**
5. **d)**
6. **b)**

REPRODUCTION

Individual organisms have limited life spans; however, life continues due to reproduction. There are two types of reproduction. One requires the exchange of genetic material between two organisms (**sexual reproduction**), and the other does not (**asexual reproduction**).

Asexual Reproduction

All kingdoms have organisms that engage in asexual reproduction. Asexual reproduction very quickly produces large numbers of genetically identical (or **cloned**) offspring. Some organisms that engage in asexual reproduction can also engage in sexual reproduction at least part of the time.

Comparison Chart

	Asexual Reproduction	Sexual Reproduction
Number of organisms involved:	One	Two
Cell division:	Mitosis	Meiosis
Variation in offspring:	No	Yes
Advantages:	Quick. No need to search for mate	Variation
Disadvantages:	No variation	Requires two organisms

In single-celled organisms such as bacteria and protists, asexual reproduction occurs through a process known as **binary fission** (or **bipartition**). The cell first duplicates parts of itself before splitting into two separate, but identical, cells. Some organisms reproduce asexually using the process of **budding**, wherein an offshoot of their body grows into a complete organism.

Many multi-cellular invertebrates can also reproduce asexually by a process called **fragmentation**, where a portion of the organism's body is separated and then grows into a whole organism. This is similar to budding, except that the original body repairs itself as well, leaving behind two complete organisms.

Plants can reproduce asexually by budding or fragmentation, when they form tubers, rhizomes, bulbs, and other extensions of their bodies. Plants also have a major sexual phase of their life cycle, which is part of a process called **alternation of generations.**

Alternation of Generations

Although asexual reproduction allows plants to reproduce quickly, most plants engage in sexual reproduction, at least part of the time. Sexually reproducing plants cycle between two distinctly different body types. The first is called the **sporophyte**, and the second is called the **gametophyte.**

An adult sporophyte (the part of the plant we see) produces spores. The spores are transported to new areas by animals, wind, water, etc. If the conditions are suitable, those spores will sprout into a **gametophyte** form of the plant, which is not usually seen. This gametophyte produces the eggs and sperm that will join to form a new sporophyte. This change from sporophyte to gametophyte represents an alternation of generations. The gametophyte generation is small and dependent upon the sporophyte generation. An oak tree, for example, is really the sporophyte generation of the plant; the gametophyte generation is contained within its flowers.

Sexual Reproduction

Sexual reproduction is when genetic material from one parent is combined with the genetic material from another, producing offspring that are not identical to either parent. Each parent produces a specialized cell called a **gamete** that contains half of his or her genetic information.

Male animals produce the smaller, more mobile gamete known as a **sperm cell**. Females produce the larger, more sedentary gamete known as an **egg cell**. When these two gametes come into contact, they fuse and combine their genetic information in a process known as **fertilization**. This can happen either externally or internally.

An example of **external fertilization** would be **spawning,** where eggs and sperm are both released into water and must find each other. **Spawning** is dependent upon each gender's reproductive cycle matching the other.

Internal fertilization is dependent upon **copulation**: the process wherein a male deposits sperm cells directly into the reproductive tract of a female. Because a medium like water cannot be used to transport gametes on land, internal fertilization is critical to land-based organisms.

Test Your Knowledge: Reproduction

1. The formation of tubers is an example of what kind of asexual reproduction?
   a) Budding.
   b) Binary fission.
   c) Bipartition.
   d) Root zone development.

2. Which of the following best describes alternation of generation?
   a) The sporophyte produces eggs and sperm that join and lead to the development of a gametophyte.
   b) The gametophyte produces eggs and sperm that join and lead to the development of a sporophyte.
   c) The gametophyte produces eggs and the sporophyte produces sperm that join to form a new plant.
   d) The sporophyte produces eggs and the gametophyte produces sperm that join to form a new plant.

3. In sexually reproducing organisms, gametes come from which parent?
   a) Only the male.
   b) Only the female.
   c) Both the male and female.
   d) Neither.

4. What is the main difference between asexual and sexual reproduction?
   a) Asexual reproduction is only for aquatic organisms.
   b) Asexual reproduction is practiced only by plants.
   c) Humans are the only organisms that utilize sexual reproduction.
   d) Asexual reproduction does not require a mate.

5. Which of the following is **NOT** a form of asexual reproduction?
   a) Fertilization.
   b) Cloning.
   c) Budding.
   d) Fragmentation.

Test Your Knowledge: Reproduction – Answers

1. **a)**
2. **b)**
3. **c)**
4. **d)**
5. **a)**

HEREDITY

A duck's webbed feet, a tree whose leaves change color in the fall, and humans having backbones are all characteristics inherited from parent organisms. These inheritable characteristics are transmitted through **genes** and **chromosomes**. In sexual reproduction, each parent contributes half of his or her genes to the offspring.

Genes

Genes influence both what we look like on the outside and how we work on the inside. They contain the information that our bodies need to make the proteins in our bodies. Genes are made of DNA: a double helix (spiral) molecule that consists of two long, twisted strands of nucleic acids. Each of these strands are made of sugar and phosphate molecules, and are connected by pairs of chemicals called **nitrogenous bases** (just bases, for short). There are four types of bases:

1. **Adenine (A)**

2. **Thymine (T)**

3. **Guanine (G)**

4. **Cytosine (C)**

These bases link in a very specific way: **A** always pairs with **T**, and **C** always pairs with **G**.

A gene is a piece of DNA that codes for a specific protein. Each gene contains the information necessary to produce a single trait in an organism, and each gene is different from any other. For example, one gene will code for the protein insulin, and another will code for hair. For any trait, we inherit one gene from our father and one from our mother. Human beings have 20,000 to 25,000 genes, yet those genes only account for about 3% of our DNA.

Alternate forms of the same gene are called **alleles**. When the alleles are identical, the individual is **homozygous** for that trait. When the alleles are different, the individual is **heterozygou**s for that trait.

For example, a child may have red hair because she inherited two identical red color genes from each parent; that would make her homozygous for red hair. However, a second child may have brown hair because he inherited different hair color genes from each parent; this would make him heterozygous for brown hair. When genes exist in a heterozygous pairing, usually one is expressed over the other. The gene which is expressed is **dominant**. The unexpressed gene is called **recessive**.

If you took the DNA from all the cells in your body and lined it up, end to end, it would form a (very thin!) strand 6000 million miles long! DNA molecules, and their important genetic material, are tightly packed around proteins called **histones** to make structures called **chromosomes**. Human beings have 23 pairs of chromosomes in every cell, for 46 chromosomes in total. The sex chromosomes determine whether you are a boy (XY) or a girl (XX). The other chromosomes are called autosomes.

Patterns of Inheritance

Biologists refer to the genetic makeup of an organism as its **genotype**. However, the collection of physical characteristics that result from the action of genes is called an organism's **phenotype.** You can remember this differentiation by looking at the beginning of each word: *geno*type is *gen*etic, and *pheno*type is *phy*sical. Patterns of inheritance can produce surprising results, because the genotype determines the phenotype.

Test Your Knowledge: Heredity

1. On paired chromosomes, two identical alleles are called:
   a) Heterozygous.
   b) Homozygous.
   c) Tetrad.
   d) Binomial.

2. The physical characteristics of an organism are known as its:
   a) Chromosomes.
   b) Genotype.
   c) DNA.
   d) Phenotype.

3. Which of the following is **NOT** a nucleotide found in DNA?
   a) Uracil.
   b) Guanine.
   c) Cytosine.
   d) Thymine.

4. The genotype describes an organism's:
   a) Appearance.
   b) Genetic code.
   c) Type of DNA.
   d) Eye color only.

5. The shape of the DNA molecule is a:
   a) Single spiral.
   b) Double spiral.
   c) Straight chain.
   d) Bent chain.

Test Your Knowledge: Heredity – Answers

1. **b)**
2. **d)**
3. **a)**
4. **b)**
5. **b)**

THE CIRCULATORY SYSTEM (CARDIOVASCULAR SYSTEM)

The cells in living organisms need to receive nutrients and have their waste products removed. Single-celled organisms are able to pass these substances to and from their environment directly through the cell membrane. However, in multi-celled organisms, these substances are transported by way of the circulatory system.

The cardiovascular system has three main parts: the heart (which is the pump in the system), the blood vessels providing a route for fluids in the system, and the blood which transports nutrients and oxygen and contains waste products.

Heart

The human heart has four chambers – right atrium, right ventricle, left atrium, and left ventricle – which separate fresh blood from the blood that is full of cellular waste.

When leaving the heart, blood travels through **arteries**. To remember this, imagine that the "a" in "arteries" stands for "away". *A*rteries carry blood *a*way from the heart. On its way to the heart, blood travels through **veins.**

The **superior vena cava** is the vein which brings blood from the body into the top right chamber of the heart. This top right chamber is called the **right atrium**. The right atrium is separated from the chamber below it by a valve, and separated from the chamber next to it by a wall of muscle tissue. The heart relaxes after each beat, which allows blood to flow from the right atrium, through the valve, and into the chamber below called the **right ventricle.**

The right ventricle sends blood through the **pulmonary arteries** to the lungs. Blood picks up oxygen in the lungs and then is moved through the **pulmonary veins** back to the upper part of the heart. But this time, it enters on the left side into the **left atrium.** Use that first-letter rule again to remember this: blood from the *l*ungs enters the *l*eft atrium.

The left atrium – like the right – is separated from the left ventricle below it by a valve. When this valve opens during the relaxed phase of the heart, blood flows into the left ventricle. This chamber has the largest and strongest muscular wall so that it can force blood into the **aorta**, which is the body's largest artery, pulling blood away from the heart to the rest of the body.

The Heart:

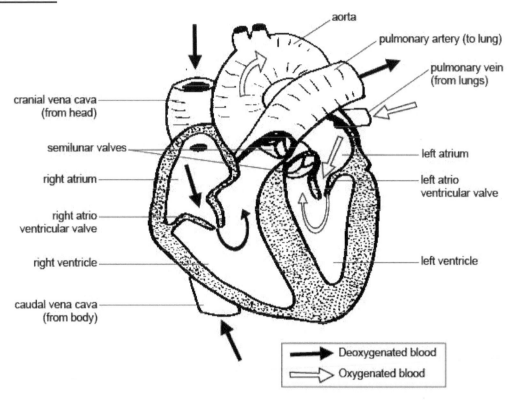

The Heart Diagram Labels:
- aorta
- pulmonary artery (to lung)
- pulmonary vein (from lungs)
- cranial vena cava (from head)
- semilunar valves
- right atrium
- right atrio ventricular valve
- right ventricle
- caudal vena cava (from body)
- left atrium
- left atrio ventricular valve
- left ventricle

Deoxygenated blood
Oxygenated blood

[4]

Arteries branch off from the aorta and travel to all parts of the body, continuing to branch and get smaller until they become **arterioles.** Arterioles lead to very small beds of tiny blood vessels called **capillaries.** Capillary beds are the site where the exchange of nutrients, gases, and wastes occurs. Blood that now contains wastes leaves the capillary beds, and enters small vessels called **venules.** These travel back through the body to the heart, becoming larger veins on the way, ending with the **large vena cava vein** that empties into the heart. This begins the cycle all over again!

Things the Circulatory System Carries:
- Oxygen from the lungs to the body's cells.

- Carbon dioxide from the body's cells to the lungs.

- Nutrients from the digestive system to the cells.

- Waste products, other than carbon dioxide, to the liver and kidneys.

- Hormones and other messenger chemicals, from the glands and organs of their production to the body's cells.

---

[4] Graphic from: http://www.en.wikibooks.org

Blood

Blood helps regulate our internal environment and keeps us in a generally constant state known as **homeostasis**. Blood transports and mixes elements up, making it possible for all the organs to contribute to maintaining homeostasis.

Blood is not a liquid; it is a **suspension** (fluids containing particles suspended inside them). Blood has two components: **plasma**, the liquid part, and the solid **blood cells** suspended throughout. There are three major types of cells: **red blood cells**, **white blood cells**, and cellular fragments called **platelets.**

Plasma
Plasma is mostly water, in which some substances such as proteins, hormones, and nutrients (glucose sugar, vitamins, amino acids, and fats) are dissolved. Gases (carbon dioxide and oxygen), salts (of calcium, chloride, and potassium), and wastes other than carbon dioxide are also dissolved in blood.

Red Blood Cells
Red blood cells contain a protein molecule called **hemoglobin**, which holds an atom of iron. The hemoglobin molecule binds with oxygen and carbon dioxide, thus providing the mechanism by which the red blood cells can carry these gases around the body.

White Blood Cells
White blood cells come in many specialized forms and are used in the immune system to fight off invading organisms and keep us from getting diseases.

Platelets
Platelets release substances at the site of a wound that start the blood-clotting reaction.

Circulation within Plants

In plants, the transport system is based on the special properties of water.

The cells that make up the vascular tissue of plants form a continuous system of tubes running from the roots, through the stems, and to the leaves. Water and nutrients flow to the leaves through a vascular tissue called **xylem**, where they are used in the process of photosynthesis. Following that process, the products of photosynthesis then flow through a vascular tissue called **phloem** back down to the roots.

Test Your Knowledge: The Circulatory System

1. Which of the following is NOT one of the chambers in the four-chambered vertebrate heart?
    a) Right atrium.
    b) Right ventricle.
    c) Left alveolar.
    d) Left ventricle.

2. Which of the following is true about blood flow in the four-chambered vertebrate heart circulatory system?
    a) Blood in the pulmonary vein is oxygenated.
    b) Blood in the pulmonary artery is oxygenated.
    c) Blood in the aorta is not oxygenated.
    d) Blood in the vena cava is oxygenated.

3. Which of the following are the major components of blood?
    a) Proteins and lipids.
    b) Plasma and cells.
    c) Proteins and platelets.
    d) Dells and lipids.

4. Platelets perform which of the following functions?
    a) Blood clotting.
    b) Carrying oxygen.
    c) Carrying carbon dioxide.
    d) Disease protection.

5. Capillary beds occur between:
    a) Arteries and veins.
    b) Aortas and vena cavas.
    c) Arterioles and venules.
    d) Atria and ventricles.

6. Red blood cells perform which of the following functions?
    a) Blood clotting.
    b) Carrying oxygen and carbon dioxide.
    c) Disease protection.
    d) Wound healing.

7. Xylem and phloem are plant tissues that:
    a) Produce sugar molecules and oxygen.
    b) Transport water and nutrients throughout the plant.
    c) Contain chloroplasts.
    d) Produce seeds.

8. The products of photosynthesis in the leaves flow to the roots through vascular tissue called:
   a) Phloem.
   b) Xylem.
   c) Meristem.
   d) Angiosperm.

Test Your Knowledge: The Circulatory System – Answers

1. **c)**

2. **a)**

3. **b)**

4. **a)**

5. **c)**

6. **b)**

7. **b)**

8. **a)**

THE RESPIRATORY SYSTEM

The human respiratory system is made up of a series of organs responsible for taking in oxygen and expelling carbon dioxide, and can be divided into two parts: **air conduction** and **gas exchange.** (We'll cover those in more detail soon.)

The respiratory system's primary organs are the lungs, which take in oxygen and expel carbon dioxide when we breathe. Breathing involves **inhalation** (the taking in of air) and **exhalation** (the releasing of air). Blood gathers oxygen from the lungs and transports it to cells throughout the body, where it exchanges the oxygen for carbon dioxide. The carbon dioxide is then transported back to the lungs, where it is exhaled.

Air Conduction

The **diaphragm**, a dome-shaped muscle located at the bottom of the lungs, controls breathing. When a breath is taken, the diaphragm flattens and pulls forward, making more space for the lungs. During exhalation, the diaphragm expands upwards to force air out.

Humans breathe through their noses or mouths, which causes air to enter the **pharynx** (upper part of the throat). The air then passes the **larynx** (the Adam's apple on the inside of the throat). The larynx is also known as the voice box because it changes shape to form sounds. Inhaled air passes into a tube in the center of the chest known as the **trachea**, (the windpipe) which filters the air.

The trachea branches into two **bronchi**, two tubes which carry air into the lungs. Once inside the lungs, each bronchus branches into smaller tubes called **bronchioles**. Bronchioles then lead to sac-like structures called **alveoli**, where the second function of the respiratory system – gas exchange – occurs.

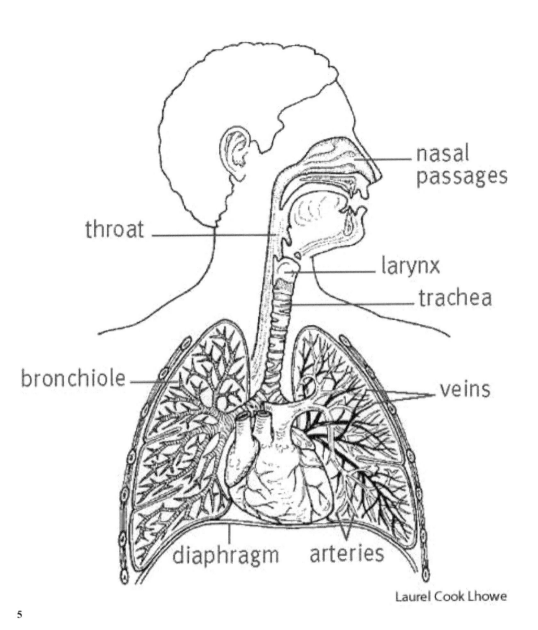

nasal passages

throat

larynx

trachea

bronchiole

veins

diaphragm   arteries

Laurel Cook Lhowe

5

[5] The American Heritage® Science Dictionary Copyright © 2010 by Houghton Mifflin Harcourt Publishing Company. Published by Houghton Mifflin Harcourt Publishing Company.

Gas Exchange

Each lung contains over two million alveoli, which creates a large surface area for gas exchange: approximately 800 square feet!

The alveoli and the surrounding blood vessels have very thin walls, which allows for the diffusion of gases in either direction – specifically oxygen and carbon dioxide. Air entering the lungs from the atmosphere is high in oxygen and low in carbon dioxide. This means that the alveoli have a high concentration of oxygen and a low concentration of carbon dioxide.

The opposite is true for the blood within the alveoli's blood vessels. Blood entering the lungs is *low* in oxygen and *high* in carbon dioxide because of cellular respiration (metabolism).

Because the alveoli have a high concentration of oxygen and a low concentration of carbon dioxide, while their blood vessels have the opposite condition, the two gases flow in opposite directions (gas exchange).

Plants exchange gas as well. Single-celled plants, like their animal counterparts, simply exchange gases through the cell membranes. Multicellular plants use pores on the leaf surface, called **stomata**, to exchange gases with the atmosphere.

Test Your Knowledge: The Respiratory System

1. The conduction of air through the respiratory system follows which of the following paths?
   a) Pharynx, larynx, alveoli, trachea, bronchus, bronchioles.
   b) Alveoli, bronchioles, bronchus, trachea, larynx, pharynx.
   c) Pharynx, larynx, trachea, bronchus, bronchioles, alveoli.
   d) Bronchus, bronchioles, alveoli, pharynx, larynx, trachea.

2. Each alveolus in the lungs is covered by tiny blood vessels to perform which of these functions?
   a) Excretion of fluids.
   b) Gas exchange.
   c) Blood production.
   d) Air intake.

3. The pores on a plant leaf that allow for gas exchange are called:
   a) Alveoli.
   b) Cell pores.
   c) Membrane gaps.
   d) Stomata.

4. Which of the following occurs during gas exchange in a cell?
   a) Oxygen is flowing from a low concentration inside the cell to a high concentration outside the cell.
   b) Oxygen is flowing from a high concentration in the red blood cells to a low concentration inside the body cell.
   c) Carbon dioxide is moving from the red blood cells into the body cells, while oxygen is moving from the body cells into the red blood cells.
   d) Carbon dioxide is flowing from a low concentration outside the cells to a high concentration inside the cells.

5. The lungs are very efficient at gas exchange because they have a:
   a) High mass.
   b) Low volume.
   c) High surface-area-to-volume ratio.
   d) Low surface-area-to-volume ratio.

Test Your Knowledge: The Respiratory System – Answers

1. c)
2. b)
3. d)
4. b)
5. c)

THE SKELETAL SYSTEM

Skeletal systems provide structure, support, form, protection, and movement. Of course, muscles do the actual *moving* of an organism, but bones – a major component of the skeletal system –create the framework through which muscles and organs connect. The bone marrow in animal skeletal systems performs **hematopoiesis** (the manufacturing of both red blood cells and white blood cells).

Skeletal systems come in many different forms - those inside of the body are called **endoskeletons**, while those skeletal structures formed outside of the body are known as **exoskeletons**. Crabs and insects have hard shells made of **chitin** to protect their entire bodies. Some organisms, such as starfish, have skeletons made up of tubes filled with fluids running through their bodies. These fluid skeletal systems are called **hydrostatic**.

Joints are where two bones come together. **Connective tissues** at the joint prevent the bones from damaging each other. Joints can be freely movable (elbow or knee), slightly movable (vertebrae in the back), or immovable (skull).

Plants also have a need for support, shape, and protection. While nonvascular do not have a great need for support (remember, they don't grow very tall), vascular plants require a great deal of support. Remember cell walls (a semi-permeable, rigid structure that surrounds each cell outside the cell membrane)? The support and structure of plant cells are primarily derived from the cell wall. Additional support and structure is provided by the tubes used to move water and nutrients through the plant.

Test Your Knowledge: The Skeletal System – Answers

1. Which of the following is NOT a function of the skeletal system in animals?
   a) Transport fluids.
   b) Produce oil.
   c) Placement of internal organs.
   d) Production of blood cells.

2. Which of the following is true of bones?
   a) They contain nerves.
   b) Some are unbreakable.
   c) They are present in vertebrates.
   d) They directly touch each other at a joint.

3. Which of the following animals does **NOT** have an exoskeleton?
   a) Insects.
   b) Crabs.
   c) Lobsters.
   d) Earthworms.

4. What type of tissue is found at joints and protects bones from rubbing against each other and becoming damaged?
   a) Contractile.
   b) Connective.
   c) Conductive.
   d) Catabolic.

5. Fluid skeletal systems are _____.
   a) Hydrostatic.
   b) Hydrolic.
   c) Hydrophobic.
   d) Hydroskeleton.

Test Your Knowledge: The Skeletal System – Answers

1. b)
2. c)
3. d)
4. b)
5. a)

THE NERVOUS SYSTEM

Irritability is a term used to describe an organism's response to changes, or **stimuli**, in its surroundings. All living organisms respond to environmental stimulus, usually by taking some sort of action: movement of a muscle, gland secretion, activating entire systems like digestion, etc.

Plants have cellular receptors that use chemical messengers to detect and respond to aspects of their environment such as light, gravity, and touch. For example, the orientation of a plant toward or away from light, called **phototropism** is mediated by hormones.

In multi-celled animals, a nervous system controls these responses.

The functioning unit of the nervous system is the **neuron**, a cell with structures capable of transmitting electrical impulses. A neuron must be able to first receive information from internal or external sources, before integrating the signal and sending it to another neuron, gland, or muscle. In multi-celled vertebrates, each neuron has four regions.

At one end of the neuron, there are branch-like extensions called **dendrites**, which receive signals from other neurons.

The **cell body** of the neuron is where the cellular functions take place and where signals are integrated.

The **axon** is an extension from the cell body which the nerve impulses travel along. Axons can be several feet in length, carrying signals from one end of the body to the other.

At the very end of the axon is the **synaptic terminal**, an area that contains chemical substances called **neurotransmitters.**

When an electrical nerve signal reaches the synaptic terminal, it causes neurotransmitters to be released. Neurotransmitters then move across the small space between the neuron and the next neuron (or gland or muscle). This small space is called the **synapse.** Once across the synapse, the neurotransmitter is received by the dendrites of another neuron (or the receptors on a gland or muscle) and then turned back into an electrical signal to be passed on.

The nervous system is divided into two main systems, the **central nervous system (CNS)** and the **peripheral nervous system (PNS)**.

CNS

The central nervous system consists of the brain and spinal cord (contained within the vertebral column or backbone). The brain integrates all the signals in the nervous system, and therefore is responsible for controlling every aspect of the body.

PNS

The peripheral nervous system consists of the nerves outside of the brain and spinal cord. The main function of the PNS is to connect the CNS to the limbs, organs, and **senses**. Unlike the CNS, the PNS is not protected by the bone of spine and skull. This leaves the PNS exposed to toxins and mechanical injuries. The peripheral nervous system is divided into the **somatic nervous system** and the **autonomic nervous system**.

The **somatic nervous system** deals with motor functions. Its nerves connect with skeletal muscle and control movement of all kinds, from fine motor skills to walking and running.

The **autonomic nervous system** works mostly without our conscious control. It is often responsible for critical life functions such as breathing and heart rate. The autonomic nervous system has two divisions.

The **sympathetic division** is responsible for the fight-or-flight response; it prepares the body for high-energy, stressful situations.

The **parasympathetic division** is responsible for rest and digestion functions, so it tends to slow down the body.

Nerves from each of these divisions usually make contact with the same organs, but they often have opposite effects.

The Endocrine System

Another important system in our body is the endocrine, or glandular, system. It controls growth rate, feelings of hunger, body temperature, and more. Many organs run the endocrine system: the **pituitary gland**, the **pancreas**, the **ovaries** (only in females) and **testes** (only in males), the **thyroid** gland, the **parathyroid** gland, the **adrenal** glands, etc.

Of all these, the pituitary gland is the most important endocrine gland in your body. About the size of a pea, the pituitary gland hangs down from the base of your brain and produces the hormone which controls growth.

Fun Fact: Humans grow faster at night because more hormones are released into your blood when you are sleeping.

Test Your Knowledge: The Nervous System

1. _____ is the functional unit of the nervous system.
   a) The nephron
   b) The nucleus
   c) The neuron
   d) The neutrophil

2. Which of the following is a part of the CNS?
   a) Autonomic nerves.
   b) Sympathetic nerves.
   c) Peripheral nerves.
   d) Spinal cord nerves.

3. What is the chemical substance that carries a message from one cell to another?
   a) Axon fluid.
   b) Dendrite fluid.
   c) Neurotransmitter.
   d) Hormone.

4. Dendrites receive information from:
   a) The axon of other neurons.
   b) The dendrites of other neurons.
   c) The cell body of other neurons.
   d) The nucleus of other neurons.

5. _____ release neurotransmitters.
   a) Axons.
   b) Dendrites.
   c) Cell bodies.
   d) The nucleus.

6. Which of the following is NOT true about irritability?
   a) Plants do not experience irritability.
   b) Activates neurons in the brain.
   c) Requires axons in animals.
   d) Neurons act upon muscles.

7. The most important gland in the human body is:
   a) The pancreas.
   b) The pituitary.
   c) The ovaries.
   d) The thyroid.

Test Your Knowledge: The Nervous System – Answers

1. c)

2. d)

3. c)

4. a)

5. a)

6. a)

7. b)

THE MUSCULAR SYSTEM

Muscles are often viewed as the "machines" of the body. They help move food from one organ to another, and carry out physical movement. There are three types of muscles in our body: cardiac, smooth, and skeletal. The nervous system controls all three types of muscle tissue, both consciously (controlled) and unconsciously (automatic).

Skeletal (or **striated**) muscle tissue is consciously controlled. The muscle is attached to bones, and when it contracts, the bones move. Skeletal tissue also forms visible muscles, as well as much of the body mass.

Smooth muscle is under automatic control and is generally found in the internal organs, especially in the intestinal tract and in the walls of blood vessels.

Cardiac muscle is found only in the heart. This type of muscle tissue is so automated that it will continue to contract even without stimulation from the nervous system. Isolated heart cells in a dish will continue to contract on their own until oxygen or nutrient sources are used up.

Muscle contraction begins when a nerve impulse causes the release of a chemical called a **neurotransmitter**. Muscle contraction is explained as the interaction between two necessary muscle proteins: thick bands of **myosin** and thin bands of **actin**. The thick myosin filaments have small knob-like projections that grab onto the thin actin filaments. As these knobs move slightly, they pull the actin filaments, which slide alongside the myosin filaments. This has the effect of shortening the muscle and thus causing a contraction.

Connective tissues known as **tendons** form a link between muscles and bones (whereas **ligaments** form a link between two bones). The contraction of a muscle causes an exertion of force upon the tendon, which then pulls its attached bone. This movement is synchronized by the central nervous system and results in movement.

Uni-cellular organisms, such as protists and sperm cells, have the ability to move as well. This kind of movement can be accomplished in three different ways. In the case of amoebas, which are one-celled formless blobs of protoplasm, movement is accomplished by extending a portion of the cell itself and then flowing into that portion. Other organisms use **cilia,** which are tiny hair-like projections from the cell membrane, or **flagellum**, which is a tail-like projection that whips around or spins to move.

Test Your Knowledge: The Muscular System

1. What are the three types of muscle cells?
   a) Cardiac, synaptic, and skeletal.
   b) Cardiac, autonomic, and smooth.
   c) Skeletal, cardiac, and smooth.
   d) Smooth, cardiac, and spinal.

2. Which of the following is true about skeletal muscles?
   a) They all contract unconsciously.
   b) All muscle movement is consciously controlled.
   c) They connect directly to one another.
   d) They are also known as striated muscles.

3. What two protein molecules are needed for muscles to contract?
   a) Pepsin and insulin.
   b) Myosin and pepsin.
   c) Hemoglobin and insulin.
   d) Myosin and actin.

4. Flagellum and cilia:
   a) Work with an organism's muscles for movement.
   b) Are parts of all cells and are required for movement.
   c) Are used by organisms without muscular systems.
   d) None of the above.

5. Peristalsis is a process performed by which type of muscle tissue?
   a) Catabolic.
   b) Cardiac.
   c) Smooth.
   d) Skeletal.

Test Your Knowledge: The Muscular System – Answers

1. c)
2. d)
3. d)
4. c)
5. c)

THE DIGESTIVE SYSTEM

Digestion involves mixing food with digestive juices, moving it through the digestive tract, and breaking down large molecules of food into smaller molecules. The digestive system is made up of the **digestive tract**: a series of hollow organs joined in a long, twisting tube that leads from the mouth to the anus. Several other organs that help the body break down and absorb food are a part of the digestive system as well.

The organs that make up the digestive tract are the **mouth, esophagus, stomach, small intestine, large intestine (colon), rectum,** and **anus**. These organs are covered with a lining called the **mucosa**. In the mouth, stomach, and small intestine, the mucosa contains tiny glands which produce juices to help break down food.

Two "solid" digestive organs, the **liver** and the **pancreas**, produce digestive juices that travel to the intestine through small tubes called **ducts**. The **gallbladder** stores the liver's digestive juices until they are needed in the intestine. The circulatory and nervous systems are also important to the digestive system.

Digestive pathway

The large, hollow organs of the digestive tract contain a layer of muscle that enables their walls to move. This movement propels food and liquid through the system and assists in mixing the contents within each organ. The movement of food molecules from one organ to the next, through *muscle action*, is called **peristalsis**.

The first major muscle movement occurs when food or liquid is swallowed. Although you are able to start swallowing by choice, once the swallow begins, it becomes involuntary (controlled by nerves).

Swallowed food is pushed into the esophagus, which connects the throat with the stomach. At the junction of the esophagus and stomach, there is a ring-like muscle (**lower esophageal sphincter**) that controls the passage between the two organs. As food approaches the closed sphincter, it relaxes and allows the food to pass through to the stomach.

The stomach has three mechanical tasks:

1. It stores the swallowed food and liquid.

2. It mixes the stored food and liquid with digestive juices produced by the stomach.

3. It empties its contents slowly into the small intestine.

Once in the stomach, the food is churned and bathed in a very strong acid (**gastric acid**). When food in the stomach is partly digested and mixed with stomach acids, it is called **chyme**. Several factors affect how long food molecules remain in the stomach, including the type of food, the degree of muscle action of the emptying stomach, and the breakdown of food occurring in the small intestine. Carbohydrates spend the least amount of time in the stomach, followed by proteins; fats remain in the stomach for the longest amount of time.

From the stomach food molecules enter the first part of the small intestine called the **duodenum**. They then enter the **jejunum**, and then the **ileum** (the final part of the small intestine). In the small intestine, **bile** (produced in the liver and stored in the gall bladder), pancreatic enzymes, and other digestive enzymes produced in the small intestine help break down the food even further. Many accessory organs such as the liver, pancreas, and gall bladder contribute enzymes and buffering fluids to the mix inside of the small intestine; this also aids in the chemical break down of food molecules.

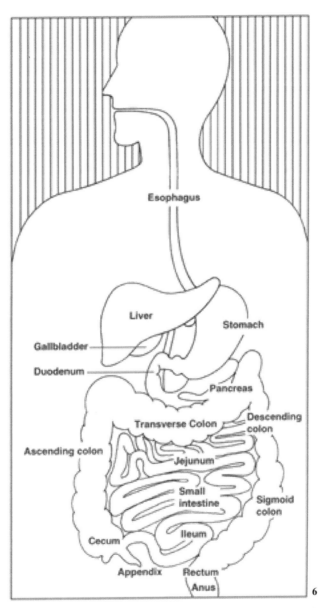

Food then passes into the large intestine, also known as the colon. The main function of the colon is to absorb water, which reduces the undigested matter into a solid waste called feces. Microbes in the large intestine help in the final digestion process. The first part of the large intestine is called the cecum (the appendix is connected to the cecum). Food then travels upward in the ascending colon. The food travels across the abdomen in the transverse colon, goes back down the other side of the body in the descending colon, and then through the sigmoid colon. Solid waste is then stored in the rectum until it is excreted.

---

[6] Graphic from: http://digestive.niddk.nih

Test Your Knowledge: The Digestive System

1. Food begins the digestive process in the:
    a) Esophagus.
    b) Stomach.
    c) Intestines.
    d) Mouth.

2. Chyme is:
    a) Water and completely broken down food molecules.
    b) Acids and completely broken down food molecules.
    c) Acids and partially broken down some food molecules.
    d) Water and partially broken down some food molecules.

3. Where is bile stored?
    a) In the pancreas.
    b) In the gallbladder.
    c) In the liver.
    d) In the small intestines.

4. Which of the following is NOT an accessory organ of the digestive system?
    a) Liver.
    b) Pancreas.
    c) Gall bladder.
    d) Urinary bladder.

5. The chief function of the colon is to:
    a) Absorb water from undigested waste.
    b) Produce sugars.
    c) Absorb protein from undigested waste.
    d) Produce carbohydrates.

Test Your Knowledge: The Digestive System – Answers

1. **d)**
2. **c)**
3. **b)**
4. **d)**
5. **a)**

THE RENAL SYSTEM (FILTRATION/EXCRETION SYSTEM)

Single-celled organisms excrete toxic substances either by diffusion through their cell membranes, or through specialized organelles called **vacuoles.** When metabolic chemical reactions occur within the cells of organisms, wastes are produced that could cause harm to the body. Those wastes therefore must be excreted. Multicellular organisms require special organ systems – humans specifically utilize the circulatory and excretory systems – to eliminate wastes.

Organisms need to be able to respond to changes in their external environment, all the while still maintaining a relatively constant internal environment. They must maintain a balance of water, temperature, and salt concentration, to name just a few. The physical and chemical processes that work to maintain an internal balance are called **homeostasis.** You may recognize this term from the previous discussion on blood and the circulatory system. Homeostasis is maintained by the cooperation of both the circulatory and the renal systems.

We have discussed digestions: food is broken down, absorbed as very small molecules, and carried to the cells by blood. Cells need these broken-down molecules to perform the life-sustaining biochemical reactions of metabolism, which produce wastes.

1. Aerobic respiration produces water and **carbon dioxide**.

2. Anaerobic respiration produces **lactic acid** and carbon dioxide.

3. Dehydration synthesis produces water.

4. Protein metabolism produces **nitrogenous wastes**, (i.e. **ammonia**).

5. Other metabolic processes can produce salts, oils, etc.

Non-toxic wastes can be retained, released, or recycled through other reactions. **Toxic** wastes however, are disposed of according to their molecular make-up. For example, blood carries gaseous wastes like carbon dioxide to the lungs for exhalation. Other wastes need to be filtered out of the blood and then excreted. Nitrogenous wastes are the result of excess amino acids broken down during cellular respiration. The toxicity (harmfulness) of those nitrogenous wastes varies from:

Extremely Toxic - **Ammonia**
Less Toxic - **Urea**
Non-toxic – **Uric Acid**

The Kidneys

Toxic wastes are carried by blood to the liver, where they are converted into **urea.** The blood then carries the urea to the **kidneys** (bean-shaped, fist-sized organs), where it will be converted from urea into **urine**. Urine is able to mix with water and be excreted from the body; the amount of water that is used in this process is regulated by the kidneys in order to prevent body dehydration.

The kidneys are complex filtering systems which maintain the proper levels of various life-supporting substances, including sodium; potassium; chloride; calcium; glucose sugar; and amino acids. These life-supporting substances are absorbed by the kidneys from urine before it I expelled. The kidneys also help maintain blood pressure and the acidity (pH) level of the blood.

Each kidney contains at least a million individual units called **nephrons.** Nephrons perform similar functions as the alveoli do in the lungs; but whereas the alveoli function as areas of gas exchange, the kidney nephrons are structured to function as areas of *fluid* interchange. Each nephron contains a bed of capillaries. Those capillaries which are bringing in blood are surrounded by a **Bowman's capsule**.

A Bowman's capsule is an important part of the filtration system in the kidneys. The capsule separates the blood into two components: a cleaned blood product, and a filtrate which is moved through the nephron. As the filtrate travels through the nephron, more impurities are removed. The filtrate is concentrated into **urine**, which is then processed for elimination. The collected urine flows into the **ureters**, which take it to the **urinary bladder**. Urine will collect in the urinary bladder until the pressure causes an urge to expel it from the body through the **urethra**.

Each nephron in the kidneys is attached to its own Bowman's capsule, and there are hundreds of thousands of nephrons. Functioning kidneys can process the blood in the body about 20 times each day, illustrating just how important these structures are. The kidneys are truly a feat of natural engineering. In fact, despite the medical community's best efforts, it has so far been impossible to build a fully artificial kidney.

Kidneys also regulate the amount of water circulating in the bloodstream. If the brain detects depleted levels of water in the blood, it increases the release of the **antidiuretic hormone (ADH)**. ADH causes the kidneys to reabsorb water into the bloodstream, which in turn concentrates the urine and preserves water for the body. The reason why you urinate more frequently when drinking alcohol is because alcohol inhibits the ADH signal from the brain.

Test Your Knowledge: The Renal System

1. The kidneys filter which of the following from blood?
   a) Undigested food.
   b) Metabolic wastes.
   c) Blood cells.
   d) Platelets.

2. Which of the following is **NOT** a function of the kidneys?
   a) Regulating pH (acidity) of blood.
   b) Regulating blood pressure.
   c) Assisting in the maintenance of homeostasis.
   d) Regulating hormone release.

3. The nephron is where _____ is produced.
   a) Urine.
   b) Ammonia.
   c) Nucleic acid.
   d) Amino acid.

4. Waste concentrated in the Bowman's capsule is called:
   a) Urine.
   b) Salts.
   c) Nucleic acids.
   d) Amino acids.

5. Alcohol consumption increases urination because it:
   a) Increases the amount of water in the body.
   b) Increases the action of antidiuretic hormone.
   c) Decreases the action of antidiuretic hormone.
   d) Stops water reabsorption.

Test Your Knowledge: The Renal System – Answers

1. **b)**
2. **d)**
3. **a)**
4. **a)**
5. **c)**

Chemistry

ELEMENTS, COMPOUNDS, AND MIXTURES

Matter

Matter is commonly defined as anything that takes up space and has mass. **Mass** is the quantity of matter something possesses, and usually has a unit of weight associated with it.

Matter can undergo two types of change: chemical and physical.

> A **chemical change** occurs when an original substance is transformed into a new substance with different properties. An example would be the burning of wood, which produces ash and smoke.

> Transformations that do not produce new substances, such as stretching a rubber band or melting ice, are called **physical changes**.

The fundamental properties which we use to measure matter are mass, weight, volume, density and specific gravity.

Extrinsic properties are directly related to the amount of material being measured, such as weight and volume.

Intrinsic properties are those which are independent of the quantity of matter present, such as density and specific gravity.

Atom

An atom is the ultimate particle of matter; it is the smallest particle of an element that still is a part of that element. All atoms of the same element have the same mass. Atomic chemical changes involve the transfer of whole atoms from one substance to another; but atoms are not created or destroyed in ordinary chemical changes.

An atom is made up of several parts. The center is called the **nucleus**, and is made up of two particles: a positively-charged particle, called a **proton,** and a particle that does not have a charge, called a **neutron**. The masses of a proton and neutron are about the same.

The nucleus of the atom is surrounded by negatively-charged particles called **electrons**, which move in orbits around the nucleus. The nucleus is only a small portion of the total amount of space an atom takes up, even though most of an atom's mass is contained in the nucleus.

Molecular Weight

A **mole** is the amount of substance that contains 6.02×10^{23} basic particles. This is referred to as **Avogadro's number** and is based on the number of atoms in C_{12} (Carbon 12). For example, a mole of copper is the amount of copper that contains exactly 6.02×10^{23} atoms, and one mole of water contains 6.02×10^{23} H_2O molecules. The weight of one mole of an element is called its **atomic weight**. The atomic weight of an element with isotopes, which are explained further on the next page, is the average of the isotopes' individual atomic weights.

The negatively-charged electrons are very light in mass. An atom is described as neutral if it has an equal number of protons and electrons, or if the number of electrons is the same as the atomic number of the atom. You may have already assumed –correctly! – from that information that the atomic number of an atom equals the number of protons in that atom. The **atomic weight** or **mass** of the atom is the total number of protons and neutrons in the atom's nucleus.

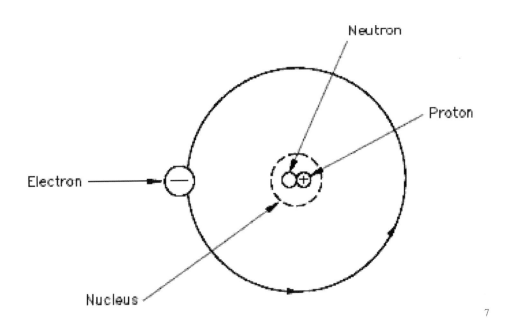

7

Elements

An element is a substance which cannot be broken down by chemical means; they are composed of atoms that have the same **atomic number** and are defined by the number of protons and neutrons they have. Some elements have more than one form, such as carbon; these alternate forms are called **isotopes.** There are approximately 109 known elements. Eighty-eight of these occur naturally on earth, while the others are **synthesized** (manufactured).

Hydrogen is the most abundant element in the Universe. It is found in 75% of all matter known to exist. **Helium** is the second most abundant element, found in approximately 25% of all known matter. The Earth is composed mostly of iron, oxygen, silicon, and magnesium, though these elements are not evenly distributed. 90% of the human body's mass consists of oxygen, carbon, hydrogen, nitrogen, calcium, and phosphorus. 75% of elements are metals, and eleven are gases in their natural state. We'll cover this more in-depth when we view the periodic table.

Molecules
A molecule is the smallest part of a substance that isn't chemically bonded to another atom. **Chemical formulas** are used to represent the atomic composition of a molecule. For example, one molecule of water contains 2 atoms of Hydrogen and 1 atom of Oxygen; its chemical formula is $2H + O = H_2O$.

---

[7] Graphic from: http://www.circuitlab.org

Compounds and Mixtures

Substances that contain more than one type of element are called **compounds.** Compounds that are made up of molecules which are all identical are called **pure substances**. A **mixture** consists of two or more substances that are not chemically bonded. Mixtures are generally placed in one of two categories:

Homogeneous mixture – Components that make up the mixture are uniformly distributed; examples are water and air.

Heterogeneous mixture - Components of the mixture are not uniform; they sometimes have localized regions with different properties. For example: the different components of soup make it a heterogeneous mixture. Rocks, as well, are not uniform and have localized regions with different properties.

A uniform, or homogenous, mixture of different molecules is called a **solution**. If the solution is a liquid, the material being dissolved is the **solute** and the liquid it is being dissolved in is called the **solvent.** Both solids and gases can dissolve in liquids. A **saturated** has reached a point of maximum concentration; in it, no more solute will dissolve.

Test Your Knowledge: Elements, Compounds, and Mixtures

1. Which statement best describes the density of an atom's nucleus?
   a) The nucleus occupies most of the atom's volume, but contains little of its mass.
   b) The nucleus occupies very little of the atom's volume, and contains little of its mass.
   c) The nucleus occupies most of the atom's volume, and contains most of its mass.
   d) The nucleus occupies very little of the atom's volume, but contains most of its mass.

2. Which of the following is not a physical change?
   a) Melting of aspirin.
   b) Lighting a match.
   c) Putting sugar in tea.
   d) Boiling of antifreeze.

3. A solid melts gradually between 85°C and 95°C to give a milky, oily liquid. When a laser beam shines through the liquid, the path of the beam is clearly visible. The milky liquid is likely to be:
   a) A heterogeneous mixture.
   b) An element.
   c) A compound.
   d) A solution.

4. The identity of an element is determined by:
   a) The number of its protons and neutrons.
   b) The number of its neutrons.
   c) The number of its electrons.
   d) Its atomic mass.

5. True or False? When a match burns, some matter is destroyed.
   a) True.
   b) False.

6. What is the reason for your answer to question **5**?
   a) This chemical reaction destroys matter.
   b) Matter is consumed by the flame.
   c) The mass of ash is less than the match it came from.
   d) The atoms are not destroyed, they are only rearranged.
   e) The match weighs less after burning.

7. An unsaturated solution:
   a) Hasn't dissolved as much solute as is theoretically possible.
   b) Has dissolved exactly as much solute as is theoretically possible.
   c) Is unstable because it has dissolved more solute than would be expected.
   d) None of the above.

Test Your Knowledge: Elements, Compounds, and Mixtures – Answers

1. d)

2. b)

3. c)

4. a)

5. b)

6. d)

7. a)

STATES OF MATTER

The physical states of matter are generally grouped into three main categories:

1. **Solids:** Rigid; they maintain their shape and have strong intermolecular forces.

2. **Liquids:** Cannot maintain their own shape, conform to their containers, and contain forces strong enough to keep molecules from dispersing into spaces.

3. **Gases:** Have indefinite shape; disperse rapidly through space due to random movement and are able to occupy any volume. They are held together by weak forces.

Two specific states of matter are **liquid crystals**, which can maintain their shape as well as be made to flow, and **plasmas**, gases in which electrons are stripped from their nuclei.

There are four physical properties of gases that are related to each other. If any one of these changes, a change will occur in at least one of the remaining three.

1. Volume of the gas.

2. Pressure of the gas.

3. Temperature of the gas.

4. The number of gas molecules.

The laws that relate these properties to each other are:

Boyle's Law: The volume of a given amount of gas at a constant temperature is inversely proportional to pressure. In other words; if the initial volume decreases by half, the pressure will double and vice versa. The representative equation is: $P_1V_1 = P_2V_2$.

Charles's Law: The volume of a given amount of gas at a constant pressure is directly proportional to absolute (Kelvin) temperature. If the temperature of the gas increases, the volume of the gas also increases and vice versa. The representative equation is: $V_1/T_1 = V_2/T_2$.

Avogadro's Law: Equal volumes of all gases under identical conditions of pressure and temperature contain the same number of molecules. The molar volume of all ideal gases at $0°$ C and a pressure of 1 atm. is 22.4 liters.

The **kinetic theory of gases** assumes that gas molecules are very small compared to the distance between the molecules. Gas molecules are in constant, random motion; they frequently collide with each other and with the walls of whatever container they are in.

Test Your Knowledge: States of Matter

1. Under the same conditions of pressure and temperature, a liquid differs from a gas because the molecules of the liquid:
    a) Have no regular arrangement.
    b) Are in constant motion.
    c) Have stronger forces of attraction between them.
    d) Take the shape of the container they are in.

2. Methane (CH4) gas diffuses through air because the molecules are:
    a) Moving randomly.
    b) Dissolving quickly.
    c) Traveling slowly.
    d) Expanding steadily.

3. Which of the following would not change if the number of gas molecules changed?
    a) Volume of the gas.
    b) Type of gas.
    c) Pressure of the gas.
    d) Temperature of gas.

4. When the pressure is increased on a can filled with gas, its volume _____.
    a) Stays the same.
    b) Increases.
    c) Decreases.
    d) Turns to liquid.

5. Equal volumes of all gases at the same temperature and pressure contain the same number of molecules. This statement is known as:
    a) Kinetic theory of gases.
    b) Charles's Law.
    c) Boyle's Law.
    d) Avogadro's Law.

Test Your Knowledge: States of Matter – Answers

1. c)
2. a)
3. b)
4. c)
5. d)

THE PERIODIC TABLE AND CHEMICAL BONDS

The Periodic table

The Periodic Table is a chart which arranges the chemical elements in a useful, logical manner. Elements are listed in order of increasing atomic number, lined up so that elements which exhibit similar properties are arranged in the same row or column as each other.

1a	IIa		IIIb	IVb	Vb	VIb		VIII		Ib	IIb	IIIb	IVa	Va	VIa	VIIa	0
1 H 1.008																	2 He 4.00
3 Li 6.94	4 Be 9.01											5 B 10.81	6 C 12.01	7 N 14.00	8 O 15.99	9 F 18.99	10 Ne 20.18
11 Na 22.99	12 Mg 24.31	IIIb IVb Vb VIb ——VIII—— Ib IIb										13 Al 26.98	14 Si 28.09	15 P 30.97	16 S 32.06	17 Cl 35.45	18 Ar 39.95
19 K 39.10	20 Ca 40.08	21 Sc 44.6	22 Ti 47.90	23 V 50.94	24 Cr 51.99	25 Mn 54.94	26 Fe 55.85	27 Co 58.93	28 Ni 58.71	29 Cu 63.54	30 Zn 65.37	31 Ga 69.72	32 Ge 72.59	33 As 74.92	34 Se 78.96	35 Br 79.91	36 Kr 83.80
37 Rb 85.47	38 Sr 87.62	39 Y 88.91	40 Zr 91.22	41 Nb 92.91	42 Mo 95.94	43 Tc 99	44 Ru 101.97	45 Rh 102.91	46 Pd 106.4	47 Ag 107.87	48 Cd 112.40	49 In 114.82	50 Sn 118.69	51 Sb 121.75	52 Te 127.60	53 I 126.90	54 Xe 131.30
55 Cs 132.91	56 Ba 137.34	57-71 see below	72 Hf 178.49	73 Ta 180.95	74 W 183.85	75 Re 186.2	76 Os 190.2	77 Ir 192.2	78 Pt 195.09	79 Au 196.97	80 Hg 200.59	81 Tl 204.37	82 Pb 207.19	83 Bi 208.98	84 Po 210	85 At 210	86 Rn 222
87 Fr 223	88 Ra 226	89-103 see below	104 Rf 261	105 Ha 260	106 Sg 263												

Legend: 12 ← Atomic number; Mg ← Chemical symbol; 24.31 ← Atomic weight

57 La 138.91	58 Ce 140.12	59 Pr 140.91	60 Nd 144.24	61 Pm 147	62 Sm 150.35	63 Eu 151.96	64 Gd 157.24	65 Tb 158.92	66 Dy 162.50	67 Ho 164.93	68 Er 167.26	69 Tm 168.93	70 Yb 173.04	71 Lu 174.97
89 Ac 227	90 Th 232.04	91 Pa 231	92 U 238.03	93 Np 237	94 Pu 242	95 Am 243	96 Cm 247	97 Bk 247	98 Cf 251	99 Es 254	100 Fm 253	101 Md 256	102 No 254	103 Lw 257

- Each box contains the symbol of the element, its atomic number, and its atomic weight.

- The elements appear in increasing order according to their atomic numbers, except for the 2 separate rows.

- The vertical columns are called **groups**. Elements within a group share several common properties and often have the same outer electron arrangement. There are two categories: the main group and the transition elements.
    - The number of the main group corresponds to the number of valence electrons.

    - Most of the transition elements contain 2 electrons in their valence shells.

- The horizontal rows are called **periods** and correspond to the number of occupied electron shells of the atom.
- The elements set below the main table are the **lanthanoids** (upper row) and **actinoids**. They also usually have 2 electrons in their outer shells.

- Most of the elements on the periodic table are metals. The alkali metals, alkaline earths, basic metals, transition metals, lanthanides, and actinides are all groups of metals.

---

[8] Graphic from: http://volcano.oregonstatevolcano.oregonstate.edu.edu

- In general, the elements increase in mass from left to right and from top to bottom.

- The main difference between the modern periodic table and the one Mendeleev (the periodic table's creator) came up with is that Mendeleev's original table arranged the elements in order of increasing atomic weight, while the modern table orders the elements by increasing atomic number.

Electronic Structure of Atoms

The electrons of an atom have fixed energy levels. Electrons in the principle energy levels are said to be in **electron shells**. Those shells which correspond to the highest energy levels include the electrons usually involved in chemical bonding. Those shells are called **valence shells**. Chemical formulas of simple compounds can often be predicted from valences. The valence electrons increase in number as you go across the periodic table.

The electrons in the outer orbit can combine with other atoms by giving up electrons or taking on electrons. Atoms that give up electrons (**cations**) change from being neutral to having a *positive* charge. Atoms that gain electrons (**ions**) change from being neutral to having a *negative* charge. The **octet rule** is a chemical rule which states that atoms of a low atomic number will share, gain, or lose electrons in order to fill outer electron shells with eight electrons. This is achieved through different types of bonding.

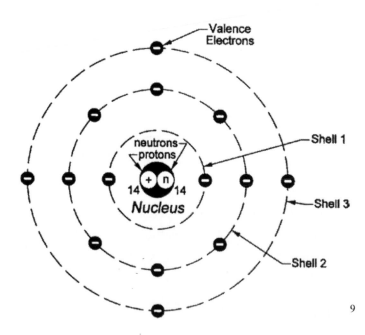

Chemical Bonds

Electromagnetism is a force that is involved in all chemical behavior, including the chemical bonds which hold atoms together in order to form molecules, as well as those that hold molecules together to form all substances. **Electronegativity** is a measure of the tendency of an atom to attract a bonding pair

---

[9] Graphic from: http://www.circuitlab.org

of electrons. Electronegativity is affected by both the atomic number and the distance between the valence electrons and the charged nucleus. The higher the assigned electronegativity number, the more an element or compound attracts electrons.

The two main types of bonds formed between atoms are **ionic bonds** and **covalent bonds.** As a result of being negatively and positively charged, anions and cations usually form bonds known as ionic bonds and exist because of the attraction of opposite charges.

A covalent bond forms when atoms share valence electrons. Atoms do not always share the electrons equally, which results in a **polar covalent bond**. When electrons are shared by two metallic atoms, a **metallic bond** can form. The electrons which participate in metallic bonds may be shared between any of the metal atoms in the region.

If the electronegativity values of two atoms are similar, then:

- Metallic bonds form between two metal atoms.

- Covalent bonds form between two non-metal atoms.

- Non-polar covalent bonds form when the electronegativity values are very similar.

- Polar covalent bonds form when the electronegativity values are a little further apart.

If the electronegativity values of two atoms are different, then ionic bonds are formed.

Most metals have less than 4 valence electrons, which allows them to either gain a few electrons or lose a few; they generally tend to lose electrons, which causes them to become more positive. (This means that metals tend to form cations.)

A **hydrogen bond** is not considered a chemical bond. Instead, in a hydrogen bond, the attractive force between hydrogen is attached to an electronegative atom of one molecule and an electronegative atom of a different molecule. Usually the electronegative atom is oxygen, nitrogen, or fluorine, which have partial negative charges. The hydrogen has the partial positive charge. Hydrogen bonds are much weaker than both ionic and covalent bonds.

Test Your Knowledge: The Periodic Table and Chemical Bonds

1. When cations and anions join, they form what kind of chemical bond?
   a) Ionic.
   b) Hydrogen.
   c) Metallic.
   d) Covalent.

2. Generally, how do atomic masses vary throughout the periodic table of the elements?
   a) They decrease from left to right and increase from top to bottom.
   b) They increase from left to right and increase bottom to top.
   c) They increase from left to right and increase top to bottom.
   d) They increase from right to left and decrease bottom to top.

3. The force involved in all chemical behavior is:
   a) Electronegativity.
   b) Covalent bonds.
   c) Electromagnetism.
   d) Ionic bonds.

4. Which one of the following is not a form of chemical bonding?
   a) Covalent bonding.
   b) Hydrogen bonding.
   c) Ionic bonding.
   d) Metallic bonding.

5. Two atoms which do not share electrons equally will form what type of bond?
   a) Metallic bonds.
   b) Polar covalent.
   c) Ionic bonds.
   d) They cannot form bonds.

6. Chemical bonding:
   a) Uses electrons that are closest to the nucleus of the atoms bonding.
   b) Always uses electrons from only one of the atoms involved.
   c) Uses all the electrons in all atoms involved.
   d) Uses the valence electrons of all the atoms involved.

Test Your Knowledge: The Periodic Table and Chemical Bonds

1. a)
2. c)
3. c)
4. b)
5. b)
6. d)

ACIDS AND BASES

pH Scale

0	0.0 Hydrochloric acid (1M)
	2.0 Stomach acid
	3.0 Lemon juice
	5.0 Urine
	6.5 Saliva
7	**7.0 Pure water**
	7.4 Blood 8.0 Pancreatic juice
	11.0 Ammonia cleansers
	13.5 Oven cleaner
14	14.0 Sodium hydroxide (1 M) [10]

acids (pH 0–7), *bases* (pH 7–14)

Acids

Naturally-occurring **acid solutions**, in which the solvent is always water, have several characteristic properties in common. They:

- Have a sour taste.

- Speed up the corrosion, or rusting, of metals.

- Conduct electricity.

- Introduce H^+ cations into aqueous solutions.

These characteristic properties can be changed by the addition of a base.

---

[10] Graphic from: http://bioserv.fiu.edu

Bases (Alkalis)

Bases don't occur in as many common materials as do acids. A few examples of bases are: lime, lye, and soap. Basic solutions:

- Have a bitter taste.

- Conduct electricity, when their solvent is water.

- Introduce OH⁻ ions into an aqueous solution.

The characteristic properties can be changed by the addition of an acid.

The acidity or basicity of a solution is expressed by **pH values**. A neutral solution is defined by the following: it has equal concentrations of H^+ cations and OH⁻ ions, and a pH of 7. Neutrality is based on the pH of pure water. The more acidic a solution, the lower the pH is below 7. The more basic the solution, the higher the pH is above 7. The pH scale is based on logarithms of base 10. (If one solution has a pH of 8 and another has a pH of 10, then there is a 10^2 or 100 fold difference between the two.)

Buffers

A **buffer** is used to make a solution which exhibits very little change in its pH when small amounts of an acid or base are added to it.

An acidic buffer solution is simply one which has a pH less than 7. Acidic buffer solutions are commonly made from a weak acid and one of its salts - often a sodium salt. A strong basic solution can be weakened by adding an acidic buffer.

An alkaline buffer solution has a pH greater than 7. Alkaline buffer solutions are commonly made from a weak base and one of its salts. A strong acid can be made weaker by adding an alkaline buffer.

The human body contains many enzymes that only function at a specific pH. Once outside of this range, the enzymes are either unable to catalyze reactions or, in some cases, will break down. Our bodies produce a buffer solution that is a mixture of carbonic acid and bicarbonate, in order to keep the pH of blood at 7.4.

Test Your Knowledge: Acids and Bases

1. One of the characteristic properties of an acid is that they introduce:
   a) Hydrogen ions.
   b) Hydroxyl ions.
   c) Hydride ions.
   d) Oxide ions.

2. A solution with a pH of 12 is:
   a) Very acidic.
   b) Neutral.
   c) Very basic.
   d) You can't have a solution with a pH of 12.

3. Buffers keep the pH of a solution from changing by:
   a) Converting strong acids to weak ones.
   b) Converting weak acids to strong ones.
   c) Converting weak bases to strong ones.
   d) More than one of the above answers is correct.

4. Proper blood pH level for humans is:
   a) 7.0.
   b) 7.2.
   c) 7.6.
   d) 7.4.

5. All of the following are properties of alkalis except:
   a) Bitter taste.
   b) Basic solutions are high conductors of electricity.
   c) Introduce OH⁻ ions into an aqueous solution.
   d) The characteristic properties can be changed by the addition of an acid.

Test Your Knowledge: Acids and Bases – Answers

1. **a)**

2. **c)**

3. **a)**

4. **d)**

5. **b)**

Physics

MOTION

Speed is a scalar quantity and is defined as distance divided by time. (Ex: miles per hour.)

Velocity is a vector quantity that describes speed and the direction of travel.

Magnitude of Acceleration is defined as the change in velocity divided by the time interval.

A **scalar quantity** is described only by its magnitude, whereas a **vector quantity** is described by magnitude and direction.

Acceleration is change in velocity divided by time; an object accelerates not only when it speeds up, but also when slowing down or turning. The **acceleration due to gravity** of a falling object near the Earth is a constant $9.8 m/s^2$; therefore an object's magnitude increases as it falls and decreases as it rises.

Newton's Three Laws of Motion

1. An object at rest will remain at rest unless acted on by an unbalanced force. An object in motion continues in motion with the same speed and in the same direction unless acted upon by an unbalanced force. This law is often called "**The Law of Inertia.**"

2. Acceleration is produced when a force acts on a mass. The greater the mass (of the object being accelerated) the greater the amount of force needed (to accelerate the object). Think of it like this: it takes a greater amount of force to push a boulder, than it does to push a feather.

3. Every action requires an equal and opposite reaction. This means that for every force, there is a reacting force both equal in size and opposite in direction. (I.e. whenever an object pushes another object, it gets pushed back in the opposite direction with equal force.)

An object's **density** is its mass divided by its volume. **Frictional forces** arise when one object tries move over or around another; the frictional forces act in the opposite direction to oppose such a motion. **Pressure** is the force per unit area which acts upon a surface.

There are **Three Important Conservation Laws** which are embodied within Newton's Laws. They offer a different and sometimes more powerful way to consider motion:

1. **Conservation of Momentum** – Embodied in Newton's first law (Law of Inertia), this reiterates that the momentum of a system is constant if no external forces act upon the system.

2. **Conservation of Energy** - Energy is neither created nor destroyed; it can be converted from one form to another (i.e. potential energy converted to kinetic energy), but the total amount of energy within the domain remains fixed.

3. **Conservation of Angular Momentum** – If the system is subjected to no external force, then the total angular momentum of a system has constant magnitude and direction. This is the common physics behind figure-skating and planetary orbits.

Energy and Forces

The energy stored within an object is called its **potential energy** – it has the potential to do work. But where does that energy come from? When gravity pulls down on an object (**gravitational energy**) the object receives potential energy. **Kinetic energy**, the energy of motion, is the energy possessed because of an object's motion.

The sum of an object's kinetic and potential energies is called the total **mechanical energy** (or, **internal energy**).

Frictional forces convert kinetic energy and gravitational potential energy into **thermal energy**. **Power** is the energy converted from one form to another, divided by the time needed to make the conversion. A **simple machine** is a device that alters the magnitude or direction of an applied force. Example: an inclined plane or lever.

Objects that move in a curved path have acceleration towards the center of that path. That acceleration is called a **centripetal acceleration.** **Centripetal force** is the inward force causing that object to move in the curved path. If the centripetal force is the action, the (opposite) reaction is an outwardly-directed **centrifugal force**.

THERMAL PHYSICS

Temperature and Heat

Heat and temperature are two different things. **Heat** is a measure of the work required to change the speeds in a collection of atoms or molecules. **Temperature** is a measure of the average kinetic energy of the atoms or molecules of a substance.

A **calorie** is the amount of heat required to raise the temperature of 1 gram of water by 1 degree Celsius. The **specific heat** of a substance is the ratio of the amount of heat added to a substance, divided by the mass and the temperature change of the substance.

The change of a substance from solid to liquid, or liquid to gas, etc., is called a **phase change**.

Heat of Fusion: The amount of heat required to change a unit mass of a substance from solid to liquid at the *melting point.*

Heat of Vaporization: The amount of heat needed to change a unit mass of a substance from liquid to vapor at the *boiling point.*

HEAT TRANSFER

Temperature Scales

There are three common temperature scales: **Celsius**, **Fahrenheit**, and **Kelvin**. Because it is based upon what we believe to be **absolute zero** (the lowest theoretical temperature possible before life ceases), the Kelvin scale is also known as the **absolute scale**.

Temperature Scale	Point at Which Water Freezes
Celsius	0° C
Fahrenheit	32° F
Kelvin	273K

The Two Mechanisms of Heat Transfer

Conduction: Heat transfer via conduction can occur in a substance of any phase (solid, liquid, or gas), but is mostly seen in solids.

Convection: Convection heat transfer occurs only in fluids (liquids and gases).

Both types of heat transfer are caused by molecular movement in the substance of interest.

WAVE MOTION (SOUND) AND MAGNETISM

Waves

Waves can be placed in one of two categories: **longitudinal** or **transverse**.

In a **transverse wave**, the motion of the medium is perpendicular to the motion of the wave; for example, waves on water. In a **longitudinal wave**, the motion of the medium is parallel to the motion of the wave. Sound waves are transverse waves.

A wave's **wavelength** is the distance between successive high points (**crests**) and low points (**troughs**). The **speed of a wave** is the rate at which it moves. **Frequency** – measured in **Hertz** (Hz) – is the number of repetitions, or cycles, occurring per second. The **amplitude** is the intensity (or strength) of the wave.

Sound

When vibrations disturb the air, they create sound waves. The **speed of a sound wave** is approximately 331m/s at 0° C. Human ears are capable of hearing frequencies between 20 to 16,000 Hz. The **decibel** (dB) scale is used to measure the loudness (amount of energy) of a sound wave. The scale starts at zero, which is the softest audio, and increases tenfold in intensity for every 10dB.

Magnetism is a force which either pulls magnetic materials together or pushes them apart. Iron and nickel are the most common magnetic materials. All magnetic materials are made up of tiny groups of atoms called domains. Each domain is like a mini-magnet with north and south poles. When material is magnetized, millions of domains line up.

Around every magnet there is a region in which its effects are felt, called its **magnetic field**. The magnetic field around a planet or a star is called the **magnetosphere**. Most of the planets in the Solar System, including Earth, have a magnetic field. Planets have magnetic fields because of the liquid iron in their cores. As the planets rotate, so does the iron swirl, generating electric currents which create a magnetic field. The strength of a magnet is measured in **teslas**. The Earth's magnetic field is 0.00005 teslas.

An electric current creates its own magnetic field. **Electromagnetism** (the force created together by magnetism and electricity) is one of the four fundamental forces in the Universe; the other three are gravity and the two basic forces of the atomic nucleus.

A magnet has two poles: a north pole and a south pole. Like (similar) poles (e.g. two north poles) repel each other; unlike poles attract each other. The Earth has a magnetic field that is created by electric currents within its iron core. The magnetic north pole is close to the geographic North Pole. If left to swivel freely, a magnet will turn so that its north pole points to the Earth's magnetic north pole.

Test Your Knowledge: Physics

1. The temperature at which all molecular motion stops is:
   a) −460 ºC.
   b) −273 K.
   c) 0 K.
   d) 0C.

2. _____is the amount of heat required to raise the temperature of 1 gram of water by 1 degree Celsius.
   a) Specific heat
   b) Heat of fusion
   c) calorie
   d) Heat of vaporization

3. An object that has kinetic energy must be:
   a) Moving.
   b) Falling.
   c) At an elevated position.
   d) At rest.

4. The amount of heat required to melt an ice cube is called:
   a) Conduction.
   b) Specific Heat.
   c) A calorie.
   d) Heat of fusion.

5. A moving object has
   a) Velocity.
   b) Momentum.
   c) Energy.
   d) All of these.

6. Heat transferred between a pot of boiling water and the air above it is an example of:
   a) Conduction.
   b) Convection.
   c) Heat of vaporization.
   d) Phase change.

7. _____ increases, decreases, or changes the direction of a force is:
   a) A simple machine.
   b) Energy.
   c) Momentum.
   d) Inertia.

8. _____ is a measure of the average kinetic energy of the atoms or molecules of a substance.

    a) Specific Heat
    b) Temperature
    c) Heat
    d) Force

9. Average speed is:

    a) A measure of how fast something is moving.
    b) The distance covered per unit of time.
    c) Always measured in terms of a unit of distance divided by a unit of time.
    d) All of the above.

10. Which of the following controls can change a car's velocity?

    a) The steering wheel.
    b) The brake pedal.
    c) Both A and B.
    d) None of the above.

11. The distance between two corresponding parts of a wave.

    a) Wavelength.
    b) Crest.
    c) Energy.
    d) Equidistance.

12. The high part of a transverse wave.

    a) Height.
    b) Period.
    c) Crest.
    d) Wavelength.

13. The magnetic field around a planet or a star is called a(an):

    a) Electromagnetic field.
    b) Magnetosphere.
    c) Magnetic field.
    d) Magnetic energy field.

14. The number of waves that pass a given point in one second.

    a) Trough.
    b) Energy.
    c) Crest.
    d) Frequency.

Test Your Knowledge: Physics – Answers

1. c)

2. c)

3. a)

4. d)

5. d)

6. b)

7. a)

8. b)

9. d)

10. c)

11. a)

12. c)

13. b)

14. d)

Made in the USA
Lexington, KY
30 November 2013